CHICAGO PUBLIC LIBRARY

R08939 38828

D1509162

HD
59
.H275
1992

Harris, Thomas L.,
  1931-

Choosing and working
  with your public
  relations firm.

$39.95

DATE			

BAKER & TAYLOR BOOKS

CHOOSING

and

WORKING

With Your

PUBLIC

RELATIONS

FIRM

Thomas L. Harris

NTC Business Books
NTC a division of *NTC Publishing Group* • Lincolnwood, Illinois USA

Library of Congress Cataloging-in-Publication Data

Harris, Thomas L., 1931–
    Choosing and working with your public relations firm/Thomas L. Harris.
        p. cm.
    1. Public relations consultants.   I. Title.
HD59.H275 1992
659.2--dc20   91–31940
                                                                                  CIP

Published by NTC Business Books, a division of NTC Publishing Group
4255 West Touhy Avenue
Lincolnwood (Chicago), Illinois 60646–1975, U.S.A.
© 1992 by NTC Business Books. All rights reserved.
No part of this book may by reproduced, stored in a retrieval system,
or transmitted in any form or by any means,
electronic, mechanical, photocopying, recording or otherwise,
without the prior permission of NTC Publishing Group.
Manufactured in the United States of America.

2 3 4 5 6 7 8 9 BC 9 8 7 6 5 4 3 2 1

Advance Praise for *Choosing & Working with Your Public Relations Firm*

"This is solid stuff. Tom Harris brings the professional's keen eye and the professor's objectivity to his subject. His counsel is worthwhile to both 'searchers' and 'pitchers.'"

> J. Neil Stalter
> Vice President & Director of Corporate
> Communications
> Eastman Kodak Company

"In this book, Tom Harris is focusing on the critical partnership between a PR firm and its potential clients. The book represents a 'must' checklist for this important relationship."

> Leo Armatis
> Vice President, Corporate Relations
> Meredith Corporation

"Any company would be well-served by reading this book—in choosing or evaluating their public relations firm. Tom Harris takes the 'mystery' out of this process, as he's been through it for a lot of years."

> Alvin Golin
> Chairman
> Golin/Harris Communications, Inc.

"Tom Harris is as good as public relations gets. He is truly the most professional practitioner I have ever worked with. I am eternally graceful to Campbell Soup for having introduced us.

> Laurel Cutler
> Vice Chairman
> FCB/Leber Katz

To my mentors, Dan Edelman, Paul Harper, Don Nathanson, and David Ofner; and my partner, Al Golin.

Their collective knowledge of what it takes to make a client-agency partnership work is reflected throughout this book.

Contents

Introduction

Why should a public relations counselor write a book that presumes to tell clients how to choose and work with a public relations firm?

Wouldn't it be more appropriate for a book of this subject to be written by a "client"—by a buyer rather than a seller of public relations services? After all, professional public relations organizations and publicity clubs have made a frequent practice of inviting clients to address the subject at their meetings. Many public relations firms conduct post mortems after they have won or lost a competitive new business pitch, giving the client not only the final vote but the final word.

Maybe that is the best reason for a counselor to write this book. We've listened and hopefully learned from our successes and our failures. We've had more experience as a participant in the new business process than have our clients. Look at it this way. A company may conduct a search for a corporate PR firm every three or four *years* or a firm to handle a PR project three or four *times* a year. On the other hand, a substantial PR firm may make a new business pitch three or four times a *month*.

We simply have more opportunities to observe the process as conducted by a variety of clients. Some of them seem to make a career of picking a PR firm, complicating the process, confusing the partcipating firms, and stretching out the search and the patience of all concerned. Others may be so casual that they give the impression that they don't take the search seriously or worse that they are on a fishing expedition.

The best clients approach the agency search in a thoughtful, well organized manner, managing the process by objectives and operating on a timetable. In other words, they approach the search as they would expect the PR firm of their choice to approach their account.

There is no one simple formula to picking a PR firm that applies to all clients in all situations but this book can suggest search guidelines and help you design a plan that fits your particular needs, identify and prioritize criteria that are important to you, and determine how well the PR firms who solicit the business meet those criteria. When you buy a PR firm, you are buying a group of people. No book can deal with the all important question of personal chemistry. A PR firm may score very well on paper but if you aren't comfortable with the people, you would be wise to pick another firm and people you like.

I have drawn on advice from clients, consultants, and PR firms, as well as thirty years of experience in public relations. Over that period I made more new business presentations than I can count or remember. I've pitched trade associations, professional societies, non-profit institutions and companies, large and small. Among the goods and services sold by these companies are air travel, automobiles, cheesecake, cereals, coffee, candy, computers, casters, curtain rods, charge cards, steel, shampoo, moisture cream, home permanents, hair spray, paint, pots and pans, smokeless ashtrays, garage door openers, dishwashers, pressure cookers, resorts, hotels, steaks, burgers, hot dogs, booze, beer, toys, games, gaming, package design, electric organs, life insurance, soup, soap, security systems, material handling equipment, tractors, overhead projectors, overseas travel, insect repellent, dog food, cat food, canned food, frozen food and food from vending machines.

No matter how well conceived, the search process does not assure that you and your agency will live happily ever after. A winning proposal may not make for a long and happy marriage. No matter how well you think you get to know each other during the solicitation process, it is essentially a sales situation and you will never really know your agency until you live with them. When you do, things may go well as planned. But sometimes they don't. You may begin to suspect that you have made a mistake, that you have chosen the wrong firm.

Divorce may be an easy answer but it's not often the best one. There must have been some good reason why you picked the firm you did in the first place. The ordeal of a new agency search and the loss of productive time needed to educate a new firm should be enough to try and make it work. A client–agency relationship requires a great deal of give-and-take. I take the position that it's worth the effort.

That's why Part Two of the book deals with how to work with your firm. It offers suggestions on how to get the best from your PR firm by keeping them involved, motivated, and challenged. It doesn't just happen. You must be prepared to manage the relationship that very importantly includes open and honest two-way communication. One of the very best ways to facilitate this is through a formal two-way evaluation process. That can prevent small dissatisfactions from snowballing into big problems. Finally, I have included some advice on how to achieve effective client–agency relationships which was the result of a dialogue between a successful public relations firm and its client, the world's largest consulting organization.

My aim in writing this book is to help you hire, and not fire, your PR firm.

Thomas L. Harris

PART I

Choosing a Public Relations Firm

Every week, in locations across the land, invitations to a unique tribal mating dance are issued to public relations firms by corporations and institutions. Corporations call this dance an "agency search." Public relations firms call it a "new business pitch." It is a dance in which the partners may have never met but during which they exchange intimate details of their business lives. It can result in a relationship that is long-term and mutually fulfilling or short-term and mutually disastrous. It also can determine whether a corporation achieves its public relations objectives and whether a public relations firm grows and prospers.[1]

CHAPTER 1

Do You Really Need Public Relations?

The question "Do you really need public relations?" is largely rhetorical. Every company, every trade association, every professional firm, every government agency, every non-profit institution has public relations. There are as many definitions of public relations as there are public relations experts, but all agree that public relations describes the relationships that an organization has with its various publics—its employees, their families, the communities in which the company does business, government agencies, non-profit recipients of corporate support, financial analysts, opinion leaders, advocates and activists, suppliers, distributors, dealers, customers, and media that transmit company messages to some or all of these groups.

Today these publics are increasingly referred to as "stakeholders." The organization has a stake in each of these publics, and each of the publics, in turn, have a stake in the organization. The word derived from "shareholder," one of the most important stakeholders of publicly owned companies. But "stakeholder" includes all groups whose attitudes and actions influence or are influenced by the corporation. Communicating with these diverse but interlocking audiences requires not only communications skills but in-depth knowledge of the needs and expectations of these discreet audiences.

Managing Your Public Relations

The question then isn't "Do you need public relations?" Like family relations, you've got them whether you want them or not. The real question is how best to manage these relationships. Public relations is widely accepted as a management function. Because it is a complex function that encompasses analysis, planning, action, communication, and evaluation, it requires specialized knowledge and skills. The organization must determine how to best harness this knowledge and skill to achieve its public relations objectives.

The subject of this book is how to hire and work with a public relations firm. Yet while many, perhaps the majority of organizations employ outside public relations counsel, others handle the PR function entirely in-house, and some do it extremely well. However, maintaining positive relationships with all of an organization's stakeholders is a complex business, and only the largest organizations can afford to maintain a department of public relations specialists to meet every public relations situation and need.

As their public relations needs expand, companies often have to weigh the relative advantages of adding corporate public relations staff or hiring outside public relations counsel. Some major companies maintain in-house corporate communications staff to handle many of their continuing public relations needs, including internal communications, community relations, corporate contributions, government relations—but employ outside public relations firms to conduct such activities as pro-active media relations programs or marketing public relations. Frequently the need to gain the understanding of and communicate effectively with certain important stakeholder groups requires specialized expertise that is not available in-house. Agencies specializing in environmental and nutrition public relations, for example, have grown to meet these client needs. The internal-external public relations mix varies from company to company.

This book will help your company manage the process, whether you maintain a continuing counseling relationship with a PR firm, use a PR firm for a specific function, or work with a variety of PR firms on a project-to-project basis.

The Objectivity Factor

One of the principal benefits of employing outside public relations counsel is the objectivity they bring to client problems.

In the view of public relations consultant Robert Ferrante:

> Firms provide a sense of healthy detachment from the everyday affairs of the corporation or organization. Detached from the emotion and internal politics of corporate life, they can often view the needs of media, or key audiences, more objectively and can react more dispassionately in conflicts. Further day-to-day experience gained from handling many clients can give it uncommon breadth and depth of knowledge and skill, particularly in specialized communications situations.[2]

One of the principal attractions of the public relations firm is its broad-based experience with a variety of clients. The PR firm brings the clients not only technical skills but its collected experience in solving similar public relations problems for other clients. It can objectively address a situation unfettered by pre-conceived corporate notions of what will or won't work. The firm can challenge entrenched public relations policies and practices that may no longer be applicable.

What Public Relations Firms Do

Public relations firms have expanded their capabilities well beyond publicity. Robert Ferrante says that his clients ask for help in finding firms that can do strategic planning, prioritize objectives, and apply specialized experience and skills in communicating with key constituents such as United States and foreign government officials, academia and the investment community, and segmented consumer groupings.[3]

The Counselors Academy of the Public Relations Society of America lists the following ways in which a public relations firm can help an organization:

- by providing an outside viewpoint or perspective
- by increasing an organization's overall visibility
- by supporting a product or an entire marketing effort
- by counseling in a crisis
- by communicating with employees
- by informing investors
- by strengthening community relations
- by acting as a liaison with government agencies
- by critiquing existing organization policies as they affect public relations goals
- by measuring and evaluating existing public relations programs
- by bringing new skills to support and augment existing public relations efforts.[4]

Publicity: A Public Relations Technique

Some companies may mistakenly equate public relations with publicity. In his *Webster's New World Dictionary of Media and Communications*, veteran public relations counselor, author, and lexicographer Richard Weiner explains that "public relations conceives and executes programs designed to achieve objectives related to specific groups (publics), goals, and strategies, utilizing publicity and other communications techniques."[5]

The desired result of a public relations program is to create a favorable image or reputation for a company or institution. One of the techniques utilized by public relations to achieve this goal is publicity—the use of information by the media because of its news value. Publicity results from proactive story placement and from the company's response to media requests for information.

Uses of Publicity

Publicity can be used as a technique to support public relations functions in a number of ways. Here are some of them:

- to announce earnings
- to attract and maintain shareholders
- to interpret company performance
- to focus attention on management excellence
- to forecast the future
- to announce and explain corporate actions
- to communicate a company's position on public issues
- to correct misconceptions about the company or its products
- to support or oppose legislation or regulatory action
- to announce mergers and acquisitions
- to announce executive appointments and changes
- to make company leaders famous
- to make the company the spokesman for its industry
- to announce environmental initiatives
- to respond to a crisis
- to defend products at risk
- to protect the company from special interest attacks
- to state the company's position in controversies
- to announce plant openings and closings
- to announce new jobs and explain layoffs
- to support the company's charitable contributions

- to communicate company-sponsored community programs
- to explain actions impacting the community
- to publicize open houses and plant tours
- to introduce new products
- to communicate new benefits of old products
- to build store traffic
- to support cause-related marketing and public service programs
- to position the company as a marketing leader
- to reinforce advertising campaigns and messages
- to build attendance at company-sponsored events

What Are Your PR Needs?

In order to decide whether or not you want to hire a public relations firm, it is first necessary to define your public relations needs.

- Are they temporary, for example, the introduction of a new product or support of a company-sponsored event?
- Are they continuous, such as communications with the company's employees?
- Do they require strategic counsel on the highest level, such as managing relationships with the government or financial community?
- Can they be handled out of company headquarters or do they require handling elsewhere, for example, in plant locations, test markets, state capitals, Capitol Hill, or Wall Street?
- Has a crisis hit the company requiring specialized experience in crisis management or damage control?
- Do you require agency brainpower and/or agency manpower?

Some clients require across-the-board service in all areas of public relations from their PR firm. Others use agencies for one or more public relations functions or on a project basis.

Counselor or Implementer

Some public relations programs require agency expertise; others primarily need "arms and legs" to execute the program.

Consultant Robert Ferrante makes the distinction between the roles of counselor and implementer of programs or projects. Public relations counselors help advise management on the appropriateness of its policies and actions as they affect the opinions, attitudes, and perceptions of key audiences. He says that clients also seek counsel in planning and strategizing communications programs to achieve their goals and objectives.

Organizations may seek counsel not only in policy matters affecting their overall reputation, but in specific matters relating to communications. Among the areas of special concern are investor relations, public affairs, crises, employee communications, corporate identity, minority relations, and consumer affairs.

While public relations firms may have been employed because of their counseling abilities in these areas, they may also be given responsibility to implement the plans they recommend. Ferrante observes that large clients tend to turn to large public relations firms that have the resources to execute as well as recommend programs in a number of specialized areas of concern.[6]

On the other hand, he points out that public relations firms sometimes function only in the role of implementer of client-conceived programs and projects or certain types of projects the firm may create expressly for the client. Jack Casey, founder of Casey Communications, the largest PR firm in Detroit, built his business by devising and selling unsolicited strategic programs addressing the public relations needs of targeted clients.

Ferrante points out that PR firms that function as implementers often operate on an ad hoc, or as needed, basis as an extension of the client's public relations staff. This role may account for much of a firm's repeat business since clients tend to use the same firm again and again. Clients invest in initial projects that thoroughly acquaint the firm with their goals, objectives, and strategies, its corporate or organizational culture, its reporting and budgeting systems, and other special considerations and sensitivities that play an important role in sustaining a healthy client/firm relationship.

He cites Bristol-Myers and Johnson & Johnson as firms that prefer to do their own creative thinking and rely on outside firms "to help with such specific functions as getting publicity for products; preparing brochures, press kits, videotapes, and other marketing communications support materials, and helping set up press conferences."[7]

Virtually all public relations firms function both as implementer and counselor. While even the largest PR firms do a great deal of implementing, Ferrante observes that this role is most frequently assumed by small- and medium-sized firms.

Other Sources of Public Relations Services

Some services that agencies offer can also be obtained from other sources. Some companies, even those employing PR firms, use free-lance writers for assignments ranging from executive speeches, to annual reports, to articles for company publications.

Speaker training is offered by many PR firms but can also be bought on a project basis from speaker training firms. There are even sub-specialties within speaker training ranging from providing help in making effective sales presentations to preparing clients for testimony before congressional committees. Most PR firms concentrate on preparing their clients to meet the media.

Some sales promotion, event marketing, and sports marketing companies offer limited public relations services. Even banks and management consultants looking for new sources of income have begun to offer communications services.

Another source for PR "jobs" is your advertising agency. Some advertising agencies, particularly those serving industrial clients, are experienced in writing and designing collateral material. There is, however, a difference between the selling copy of a promotion piece and a brochure that sets forth the company's position on environmental issues, for example. Many large ad agencies that routinely turn out great television commercials are stymied by long information brochure copy. The old definition of advertising ("salesmanship in in print") has now been extended to include the electronic media, but the good advertising copywriter is trained to apply writing to make a sale, rather than to increase understanding.

Jack O'Dwyer, editor of *Jack O'Dwyer's Newsletter*, warns of the problems that can arise when ad agencies get into the PR selection process.

O'Dwyer knows whereof he speaks. He spent years covering the ad industry for the old *New York Journal-American* and *Ad Daily*. He says that advertising agencies may insist on setting grand marketing strategy, turning PR into a mere echo of the ad campaign, or eliminating PR altogether. According to O'Dwyer:

> The PR campaign does not always have to dovetail with the ad campaign. In fact, some companies prefer completely different ad and PR campaigns. Advertising should never dominate PR although there are plenty of PR firms that will allow this in order to keep on the good side of the ad agency. You, the client, must prevent the firm from being squashed . . . The ad agency, knowing that PR is dealing with an uncontrollable third party (the press) may seek to inhibit PR input. The traditional ad agency fear is that a multi-million dollar campaign may be jeopardized by a PR account worth a few hundred thousand. Also remember that ad agencies traditionally have used PR as a come-on for an ad budget. PR becomes the foot in the door for a much more expensive media ad campaign . . . Be suspicious if the PR wing of an ad agency keeps trying to sell you on an ad campaign.[8]

Clients should beware of ad agencies that offer to "do PR" as an add-on accommodation for advertisers. Public relations is a labor-intensive activity that agencies can ill-afford to give away. Those ad agencies that have professional PR operations or PR subsidiary companies charge competitively for their services.

What Do You Want from Your PR Firm?

If, after considering alternate sources of PR services, internal as well as external, you determine a need for a PR firm, you should have a clear idea of what it is that you want from that firm. Do you want counsel? Or execution? Or both? Do you want a partner or a vendor? In fairness to the PR firms, you should be clear. During the selection process you will find that although most PR firms will want to give you the best of their thinking as well as their skills, they will be flexible enough to adapt to your needs.

A true partnership requires in-depth personal involvement from senior agency staff. In this regard, PR firms operate much like law firms. When you need senior legal counsel, you pay for it. The same is true for senior public relations counsel. The follow-up work can be done by lower cost people.

Long-Term Relationship or Short-Term Project?

Similarly, you should decide if you want a continuing "retainer" type relationship with a PR firm or to use a firm for short-term projects or spot assignments.

In recent years, there has been a proliferation of project or "spot assignments." While PR firms understandably prefer on-going relationships with their clients, the changing market for PR services mandates that they take on projects that have a beginning and an end. This requires greater flexibility in staffing since on-going clients have a right to expect staff continuity. Clients hiring a PR firm for spot projects must recognize that agency staff must be borrowed from existing clients.

Since PR firms must maximize utilization of staff in order to achieve their profit objectives, they can't keep a fully staffed "bullpen" of talented pros ready and waiting to handle projects on short notice. Some sophisticated clients recognize this and manage to reserve agency staff by assigning a continuing series of projects to the agency. By so doing they, in effect, achieve the same benefits of continuity as an on-going account.

On the other hand, clients impressed with the overall capabilities of a PR firm may prefer to have their own team of dedicated account people rather than borrow staff from another account group. This arrangement assures clients that their assignment will be the account group's top priority.

While spot assignments may be disruptive, most PR firms are happy to take them. They have found these projects to be profitable plus-business. Then too there is always the sometimes stated and often assumed possibility that successful performance will lead not only to other projects but to an on-going client relationship most desired by PR firms.

Some clients believe in dangling a carrot—offering the promise of more business to come. Others believe the project at hand should be considered an end in itself. This is particularly true when a product marketing group is the client. Their careers may hinge on a successful product launch. They want a firm that can help them meet their marketing objectives and are often willing to pay a premium price. Their focus may necessarily be short-range and they may, in fact, have no other perceived needs for a public relations firm.

PR firms must decide how candid they should be about their long-term aims in soliciting a project. Years ago, my firm rarely took on spot jobs because we felt that it was unfair to borrow staff from on-going clients who paid the rent. But on occasion, we competed for spot assignments when we felt there was a good opportunity for a longer-term payoff. When one beer company asked us why we wanted a small project introducing a new product in a few test markets, we told them candidly that we saw it as an opportunity to impress them with our capabilities to be their national PR firm for all occasions. They were impressed by our frankness and awarded us the business. A few years later, by coincidence, another brewery asked us why we would be interested in handling the local rollout of their primary product line. We gave them the same answer and were summarily eliminated from the competition. In this case, as we learned later, the PR program was being financed by the local distributors who couldn't have cared less about our interest in handling the account nationally. To them, local sales was the whole ballgame.

One or More PR Firms?

Some companies retain corporate PR counsel but hire other PR firms for special assignments because the new assignment requires specialized expertise or because they don't want to deter the principal firm from its primary assignment. The group dynamics of some companies also lead to agency assignments. For example, the marketing manager whose career is riding on the success of a new product introduction may hire his or her "own" agency whose efforts are totally focused on the success of the particular project. From the agency point of view, this is an opportunity to "ride a winner." The implicit promise is that as the manager rises in the company, he or she will take the successful agency along.

It is not uncommon for a large client company to have several PR firms. In addition to a corporate "agency of record" and one or more marketing PR firms, it might retain specialist firms in such areas as crisis management, investor relations, government relations, or environmental public relations.

In addition, many large companies make extensive use of local PR firms or individuals. They are often used for community relations projects and to supplement the work of the PR department. These locals are readily available to take on writing and other assignments when the department is overloaded. They are often used when budget cannot accommodate more expensive national agencies.

References

1. A.C. Croft, "Anatomy of an Agency Search," *Public Relations Journal* (September 1989), 36.

2. Robert L. Ferrante, "Using a Public Relations Firm," In Bill Cantor, *Experts in Action: Inside Public Relations*, (White Plains, N.Y.: Longman, Inc., 1989), 393.

3. Ibid.

4. Counselors Academy, *Selecting a Public Relations Firm*, Public Relations Society of America booklet, 1986.

5. Richard Weiner, *Webster's New World Dictionary of Media and Communications*, (New York: Simon & Schuster, Inc., 1990), 381.

6. Ferrante, "Using a Public Relations Firm," 393.

7. Ibid.

8. Jack O'Dwyer, "How to Hire and Get the Most from Outside PR Counsel," *O'Dwyer's Directory of Public Relations Firms 1991*, (New York: J.R. O'Dwyer Co., 1991), 139.

CHAPTER 2

Preparing for the Search

Once the need for hiring outside PR counsel is determined, the next important step is to identify and prioritize your organization's corporate goals. The Counselors Academy of the Public Relations Society of America points out that these corporate goals will become the basis for determining the organization's public relations goals. The public relations firm you choose will use them to develop strategies, tactics, and tasks specifically oriented to your management's needs.

The Counselors Academy recommends that companies construct an informal "backgrounder" as a goal-focusing exercise. The backgrounder would briefly cover the following:

- history of your organization (when founded, size, products, services, etc.)
- mission, aims of the organization
- public relations needs as presently perceived
- public relations expectations
- special public relations skills/resources sought
- current or past public relations efforts
- requirements for collateral materials; advertising, etc.
- budget commitment/parameters, if any

- initial length of contract with selected firm
- special circumstances that would affect any aspect of a public relations program[1]

Developing this information at this early stage has two important benefits. It help you better define the nature and scope of your public relations needs which, in turn, can serve as a guideline to help you know what strengths and qualities to look for in a public relations firm. These guidelines then can be used to explain your expectations to prospective firms, enabling them to direct their response to your particular needs.

Selecting the Selection Committee

After the drill of defining corporate PR goals has been completed, the next step is to choose the members of the selection or search committee. Consultant Tom Leighton, who helps companies find PR firms, believes that the smaller the search committee, the better. He told Jack O'Dwyer that:

> Too often, the search for a PR firm is viewed as a semi-social occasion, an opportunity for deserving executives to enjoy a number of agency dog-and-pony shows in the big city. Almost invariably, the committee sees too many agencies in too little time and winds up choosing the winner in a blur of fatigue.[2]

Member selection is critical since the committee's work will impact the corporation long after its mission has been completed. The composition of the committee will differ from company to company and from PR assignment to PR assignment. Whatever the circumstances, it is important that the committee include those people that will work most closely with the PR firm that is finally selected. It is important to make certain that all members of the committee will be available to participate in every step of the selection process from setting criteria to final presentation.

The Role of Top Management

The search committee that conducts the screening process will very likely be augmented at the final presentation by a wider group of company executives, including top management. This is especially true if the firm is picking a PR firm that will have broad responsibility for the corporate public relations program. In this situation, the chief executive, operating, and financial officers of the company should and usually do participate. These key executives plus the company's top public relations officer will be those most affected by and involved with the work of the corporate public relations firm.

This key group, and often the chief legal counsel, will also be involved in selecting a firm with a more immediate and limited charter of handling an emerging crisis situation, for example the response to a disaster, defense against a shareholder challenge to management, or strategically planning to address emerging issues impacting the company's mission.

For more limited public relations assignments, the involvement of top management is largely a reflection of the degree of interest in the specific area of the assignment. A marketing-oriented CEO may want to personally participate in the process of picking a PR firm to handle companywide marketing PR programs, those for a division, or even brand specific programs—especially the introduction of an important new product that will significantly affect the company's fortunes. This is especially true in small- to mid-sized companies where a "hands-on" CEO participates in company operations across the board.

Some companies may adopt a media relations strategy that focuses on the person behind the company's success. This may be especially important for new and emerging companies. The original publicity efforts for McDonald's and Sara Lee were focused on their innovative founders, Ray Kroc and Charles Lubin.

It also holds true for some of our largest companies. Lee Iacocca at Chrysler, Steven Jobs at Apple and NeXT, and Michael Eisner at Disney play key roles in the publicity for their company's major products. Ford's success with the Taurus was tied to the success of "Team Taurus" led by Ford's then-CEO, Donald Petersen.

The Marketing PR Search Committee

The selection committee for a marketing public relations firm likely will include members of the chain of marketing command from product managers or even assistant product managers up to the chief marketing officer of the company, division, or business unit.

Other members of the selection team for marketing-oriented programs might include marketing services, promotion, market research, and for some products, home economics managers. If the client company has an in-house advertising agency, its executives might also be included. If the company is organized into business units, the key player on the selection committee is the unit's general manager.

A marketing public relations search team is also likely to include the company's chief public relations officer and other members of the corporate PR (or, as it is alternately known, corporate communications or public affairs) staff assigned to the division or business unit. The role of the PR department varies from search to search. In some instances, the department initiates and manages the search, provides the deciding vote, and becomes "the client" after the agency is chosen. In others, the department plays a supporting role, recommending PR firms to be considered and aiding the selection committee by evaluating agency capabilities from a professional viewpoint.

Other PR Searches

The nature of the PR assignment will suggest other important members to be added to the selection committee. Technical products, For example, will usually necessitate the involvement of engineers, scientists, researchers, or designers if only to brief the agencies and evaluate their ability to handle technical information and their understanding of the specific assignment.

An employee relations assignment would surely involve personnel or human resource management.

An investor relations assignment, whether a broad program or a specific one such as the writing of the annual report, would require the participation of the likely client contact for the program, the company's chief financial officer, and members of the client's staff.

A government relations program usually involves close coordination between the company's lobbying and public relations activities. The search team might include lawyers and lobbyists.

Uses of a Search Consultant

Many companies, especially those who are inexperienced in working with public relations firms, employ consultants to help them conduct a search. A number of experienced public relations executives in New York, Chicago, Los Angeles, and elsewhere have become consultants to both clients and PR firms.

Some clients ask the consultant to sit in on the presentations and render an opinion. However, it is the client and not the consultant that must live with the decision. The wise consultant sets up a process that will enable the company to pick a firm that satisfies its particular requirements and with whom it is comfortable. The consultant may point out certain professional strengths or weaknesses to help a company inexperienced in public relations reach an informed decision.

Former counselor Edward Gottlieb, who now helps clients conduct PR searches, charges between $3,000 and $15,000 per search. He typically conducts the initial research and presents the client with five or six firms to consider. Together they narrow the list to three firms from which the client makes the final choice. Part of Gottlieb's service is to monitor the selected firm's performance for the first few months to make sure it gets off to a good start.

The benefits of using a PR consultant are virtually identical to those listed by advertising consultant William Weilbacher in his book

"Choosing and Working with Your Advertising Agency." He lists these six contributions a qualified consultant can make to agency search and selection:

1. An experienced consultant can direct the total search and selection process in a way that will assure the client that it has been exposed to the very best agencies available to work with on its account.

2. The consultant can assure the objectivity of the search process.

3. The consultant will know a lot more about many agencies than even the most knowledgeable clients.

4. The consultant can act as an intermediary between the client and the agency community, thus protecting the client from much time-consuming contact with a host of candidate agencies during the search process.

5. The consultant can handle all of the detailed work and contact with prospective agencies that any agency search entails.

6. The consultant knows how to make the candidate agencies show the client what it should see to make a knowledgeable appraisal of the candidates instead of an appraisal based only upon what the agencies want the client to see.[3]

Once you have determined your public relations needs, have decided that you need a public relations firm, have decided whether or not to use a consultant, and have identified your selection committee, the next step is to determine what kind of public relations firm is best suited to meet your needs. The next chapter will help you in this screening process.

References

1. Counselors Academy, *Selecting a Public Relations Firm*.

2. O'Dwyer, "How to Hire and Get the Most from Outside PR Counsel," 142.

3. William M. Weilbacher, *Choosing and Working with Your Advertising Agency*, (Lincolnwood, Ill.: NTC Business Books, 1991), 42.

CHAPTER 3

Creating the Long List of PR Firms

To identify the right PR firm for your company, you must first address several factors that are unique to your company and your needs. You should start by asking several basic questions.

Do you need a full-service PR firm or a specialized firm?

What is the right-size PR firm for you?

Is the location of the firm important?

Where do you need geographic coverage?

Does the firm have conflicts with other clients?

Full-Service or Specialized Firm

If you are hiring a PR firm to handle a broad range of public relations activities on behalf of your company, you will probably want a full-service, public relations firm. On the other hand, you may find the expertise to handle a very specific public relations problem in a PR firm that limits its practice to the specialized area you need.

A full-service firm should be able to provide you with help in all major areas of public relations. These are:

- media relations
- employee relations

- government relations
- community relations
- investor relations
- crisis communications
- issues management
- marketing public relations

The across-the-board expertise in all these basic areas of public relations will vary from agency to agency. The giant public relations firms today encompass a collection of specialized practice areas. The choice between a full-service firm and a specialized firm may not always be apparent. You may get a better feel for the relative benefits of choosing a full-service public relations vs. a specialist firm by including both in the first phase of agency screening. While most of the larger agencies have experience in each of these areas, many are stronger in some over the others. All full-service agencies offer marketing public relations, but while it is a specialty with some, it is only a sideline with others. There was no better media relations firm than Carl Byoir & Associates but, as I discovered when my company, Foote, Cone & Belding, acquired Byoir, the firm's approach to marketing public relations was usually limited to product publicity.

Specialist Firms

While most of the larger PR firms and all firms that describe themselves as full-service firms conduct corporate media relations programs and write annual reports, only a few have real expertise in the vital area of mergers and acquisitions. If your company is aggressively pursuing an acquisition target or defending against a hostile takeover, the list of qualified full service agencies truly capable of masterminding the PR component of this kind of life-and-death situation shrinks considerably. You may want to consider engaging an investor relations specialist firm for this critical assignment even if you already employ a full-service agency.

Your present public relations needs may call for a limited-service specialist firm rather than a full-service firm. There are PR

firms specializing in each of the general areas of public relations
listed previously. In addition, there are firms (and divisions of full-
service firms) whose area of expertise lies in more specialized areas.
For example, there are successful firms whose total practice is
focused in such areas as:

high-tech	food/nutrition
biotech	beauty and fashion
healthcare/medical	home furnishings
pharmaceutical	entertainment PR
quality assurance	restaurant
environment	retail
agribusiness	franchise companies
lobbying	speaker training
grassroots coalitions	sports
travel and tourism	non-profit institutions

There are even subspecialties within the non-profit public
relations category such as hospital PR and public relations for cultural and academic institutions. The unlikely locale of Keene, New
Hampshire, is the home of three competing public relations firms
that specialize in conducting public relations programs for colleges
and universities.

What Size Firm Is Right for You?

The size of the public relations firm is often a critical factor in
agency selection. In public relations, one size definitely doesn't fit
all. If you are a large company, the PR firm's record in representing
firms your size is an indication of its capability to handle your
account. That's why many large companies make what they consider
to be the safe choice of one of the large PR firms. On the other
hand, you may want to be the biggest fish in a small pond and decide
to take a chance on a mid-sized or smaller firm. You could get great
work and great service by giving a hungry and otherwise qualified

firm its first opportunity to move up to the big time. If you do choose a smaller firm, you should be convinced that the firm or its key players have the capabilities if not the direct experience your assignment calls for. You can be too big for the firm. They may be superb at doing certain kinds of PR work but lack the resources to handle all of your public relations requirements. You don't want an agency to "go to school" on you.

Whatever size firm you choose, it is important to assess the relative importance of your account to the firm. Try to avoid being a little fish in a big pond. Your chances of getting good service are likely to be commensurate with your contribution to the PR firm's overall book of business. Don't make the mistake of going with one of the largest PR firms because you are impressed by its prestige. You are hiring a firm to do a job, not to impress your friends.

It is up to you to decide if it's more important to keep all your PR work with one firm or to allocate assignments to two or more agencies who have the skills and resources to do some but not all the work. Today, as with advertising agencies, most large companies use more than one PR firm. Often the mix includes a large full-service "agency of record" and smaller firms for specialized assignments.

Geographic Considerations

The nature of the PR account and the client's style of doing business will help determine the importance of geographical considerations. The client must determine if day-to-day contact, in-depth client involvement, and close supervision is required. For other assignments, the PR firm is expected to execute the agreed on program on its own with relatively little client involvement.

Another major consideration is the perceived geographic reach of the program. Some programs are locally focused. Others require handling regionally, in major markets nationally, in widely dispersed test markets, or in global markets. A PR firm which might be the best for you locally or regionally may not be appropriate for an international program.

O'Dwyer's Directory: The Indispensable Source

Drawing up your long list of potential candidates requires you to research the universe of PR firms that meet your requirements for full or specialized service, size, location, and geographic coverage.

The best place to start is with *O'Dwyer's Directory of Public Relations Firms*, published by J.R. O'Dwyer Co., Inc., 271 Madison Avenue, New York, New York 10016. It is the single most important source of information about public relations firms. O'Dwyer's lists more than 1,800 PR firms and public relations departments of advertising agencies and their branches. Each listing includes name, address, phone and fax number, whether independently- or advertising-owned, founding date, areas of specialization, key executives, and current client list.

O'Dwyer lists the 50 largest PR firms, the 80 largest independent PR firms, and the 50 largest PR firms owned by advertising agencies. The directory also lists the leading firms that had the largest percentage gains in net fee income in the previous year. The annual rankings have been one of the most important new business sources of the larger PR firms. The CEO of one firm told me that the number of clients that asked his agency to participate in competitive solicitations increased 50 percent the year the agency moved into the top ten on O'Dwyer's list.

The following O'Dwyer lists will be of particular interest to some client companies:

- geographical index of PR firms by country, state, and city
- regional rankings by net fee income
- index to public relations firms with specialized skills

There are 18 categories listed in the most current directory:

agribusiness	financial PR/investor relations
beauty and fashion	
books and publications	foods, beverages
educational institutions	foreign markets
entertainment/theater	health

high-tech/industrial	professional services
home furnishings	society
minority markets	sports
political candidates	travel

The lists of the 50 largest PR firms, city and regional firms, and areas of specialization from the 1990 O'Dwyer's Directory of PR Firms are reproduced on the following pages with permission of the publisher for illustration purpose only. The directory is published every spring. Since agency rankings, areas of specialization, and especially client lists change significantly from year to year, it is imperative to use the current directory for researching your long list.

Importance of Client Retention and Growth

Jack O'Dwyer advises clients using his directory to look for firms that are growing, because failure to grow could mean that clients are not overly happy or are at least not recommending the firm to others. Further, he suggests comparing the firm's current client list with those of previous years.

> See how many clients the firm has been able to keep . . . . The agency should be able to show a continuing relationship with a good number of clients. Ask them for an up-to-date list of clients. The list should closely match the one in the current directory. If too many clients are suddenly missing, you can wonder how much fiction was in the original list and whether misrepresentation is a habit of this agency . . . . If most of the "current clients" turn out to be past (and sometimes long past) clients; if much of the work done was minor projects; if "staff members" turn out to be free-lancers or future employees being "lined up" if your account comes in; if "branches" turn out to be affiliates over which the agency has little if any control—then the best advice is to quickly move on to the next contender. It's better to deal with an agency that candidly describes itself—no matter how humble that reality may be—than deal with one that manufactures dreams.[1]

Other Sources of Information About PR Firms

Among the other trade sources for information about PR firms are:

- **The J.R. O'Dwyer Company,** 271 Madison Avenue, New York, 10016, (212) 679-2471, publisher of *O'Dwyer's Directory of Public Relations Firms*; also publishes *O'Dwyer's PR Services Report*, a monthly magazine which has a special issue that summarizes the directory's agency lists. Another special issue describes PRSA and IABC award-winning programs.

  O'Dwyer also produces a set of videotapes in which top executives and staffers of the ten largest PR firms are interviewed. The 25-minute agency interview tapes are available for $50 per tape. A 45-minute tape with highlights of all ten is also available for $35.

- **The Public Relations Register,** a division of The Advertising Agency Register, Inc., 155 East 55th Street, New York, 10022, (212) 644-0790, has agency videotapes of 50 top public relations firms. For a service fee of $1,500, a client can selectively view taped and written credentials presentations from participating PR firms. This service is particularly valuable for clients who do not want others to know that they are in the process of selecting a PR firm.

- **Inside PR,** a trade publication located at 235 W. 48th Street, New York, 10036, (212) 245-8680, publishes "PR Agency Yellow Pages," listing more than 2,000 public relations agencies in the United States and Canada. Agencies are listed by geographic location, by 24 specialist services, and by clients and senior personnel.

- **Inside PR** also publishes a special "Agency Report Card" issue which grades agencies on the judgment of the editors and industry sources. Its "PR All-Stars" and "Creativity in Public Relations Awards" special issues spotlight outstanding agency and client executives and programs.

<u>1990 PR FEE INCOME OF 50 FIRMS SUPPLYING DOCUMENTATION TO O'DWYER'S DIR. OF PR FIRMS</u>

(A) means ad agency related

	1990 Net Fees	Employees	% Fee Change from 1989
1. Shandwick	$210,891,000	2,112	+17.8
2. Hill and Knowlton (A)	196,700,000	1,900	+20.0
3. Burson-Marsteller (A)	190,000,000+	2,000+	+11.7
4. Ogilvy Public Relations Group (A)	62,341,000	759	+7.9
5. Omnicom PR Network (A)	61,849,214	761	+27.5
6. Edelman Public Relations Worldwide	45,970,535	495	+28.7
7. Fleishman-Hillard	45,858,000	509	+20.6
8. Ketchum Public Relations (A)	42,300,000	401	+18.4
9. Manning, Selvage & Lee (A)	29,322,000	303	+9.6
10. Ruder Finn	25,294,808	296	+19.4
11. GCI Group (A)	21,949,740	267	+35.0
12. Robinson, Lake, Lerer & Montgomery (A)	20,484,000	146	+10.0
13. Cohn & Wolfe (A)	14,998,000	122	+29.0
14. Financial Relations Board	9,540,626	110	+8.0
15. Corporate Communications (U.S.)	8,428,124	73	+9.7
16. The Kamber Group	7,422,129	100	+23.9
17. Gibbs & Soell	7,195,723	81	+4.5
18. Stoorza, Ziegaus & Metzger	6,232,017	78	+27.5
19. Earle Palmer Brown Cos. (A)	5,665,104	62	+17.6
20. E. Bruce Harrison Co.	5,618,403	49	+28.3
21. Dix & Eaton	4,800,731	47	+15.1
22. Padilla Speer Beardsley	4,481,600	49	+18.9
23. Dewe Rogerson (U.S.)	4,444,000	43	+83.0
24. The Rockey Company	4,255,381	56	+5.0
25. Cone Communications	4,228,784	46	+9.3
26. Nelson Communications Group	4,154,413	44	+38.4
27. Aaron D. Cushman and Assocs.	3,775,848	47	-6.6
28. Lobsenz-Stevens	3,700,000	40	+5.0
29. Morgen-Walke Assocs.	3,638,767	32	+16.4
30. Cunningham Communications	3,475,945	34	+38.9
31. Edward Howard & Co.	3,452,700	37	+11.0
32. Bader Rutter & Assocs. (A)	3,325,099	40	+24.2
33. Makovsky & Co.	3,300,000	40	+12.0
34. Public Communications	3,265,534	40	-2.1
35. KCS&A Public Relations	3,243,000	34	-1.6
36. Dye, Van Mol & Lawrence	3,060,571	56	+11.9
37. Clarke & Co. (A)	3,054,234	33	+17.0
38. DeVries Public Relations	3,038,701	38	+12.1
39. BMc Strategies	2,802,906	19	-8.6
40. Cerrell Associates	2,674,271	29	+18.8
41. Pacific West Communications Group	2,655,652	28	+104.0
42. Creswell, Munsell, Fultz & Zirbel (A)	2,640,717	26	-9.2
43. Charles Ryan Associates	2,526,767	39	-2.0
44. Gross Townsend Frank Hoffman (A)	2,500,000	32	+39.0
45. Bob Thomas & Associates (A)	2,500,000	30	+47.0
46. Holt, Ross & Yulish	2,495,355	31	-6.7
47. PRx	2,475,109	30	+19.0
48. M. Silver Associates	2,430,918	23	+29.9
49. Franson, Hagerty and Assocs.	2,423,000	20	+5.0
50. MWW Strategic Communications	2,399,245	18	+58.8

© *Copyright 1991 by the J.R. O'Dwyer Company, Inc.*

CITY AND REGIONAL FIRMS SUBMITTING DOCUMENTATION TO O'DWYER'S DIRECTORY OF PR FIRMS

NEW YORK

Firm	1990 Fee Income	Empl.
1. Burson-Marsteller	$50,000,000	484
2. Hill and Knowlton	45,000,000	411
3. Ogilvy PR Grp.incl. Adams & Rinehart	22,874,000	180
4. Ruder Finn	20,506,600	233
5. Robinson, Lake including Bozell PR	12,700,000	80
6. Edelman PR Worldwide	12,536,003	108
7. Omnicom headed by Porter/Novelli	12,467,937	140
8. Ketchum Public Relations	10,600,000	115
9. Manning, Selvage & Lee	10,518,000	101
10. Corporate Communications including Georgeson and Donley Comms.	8,428,124	73
11. Dorf & Stanton Comms. of Shandwick	8,125,000	94
12. GCI Group	7,084,000	70
13. Fleishman-Hillard	6,690,000	70
14. Cohn & Wolfe	6,222,000	62
15. Dewe Rogerson	4,444,000	43
16. Lobsenz-Stevens	3,700,000	40
17. Morgen-Walke Assocs.	3,638,767	32
18. Makovsky & Co.	3,300,000	40
19. KCS&A Public Relations	3,118,000	38
20. DeVries PR	3,038,701	38
21. Gibbs & Soell	2,884,856	37
22. Financial Relations Board	2,511,093	25
23. Gross Townsend Frank Hoffman	2,500,000	32
24. M. Silver Associates	2,430,918	23
25. Ayer Public Relations	2,396,139	25
26. Wang Associates	2,036,064	20
27. Brouillard Communications	2,028,000	16
28. Lou Hammond & Associates	1,883,990	25
29. Sumner Rider & Assocs.	1,868,529	21
30. Patrice Tanaka & Co.	1,473,000	15
31. G+A Communications	1,403,000	19
32. Lee Laino Associates	1,400,000	18
33. The Newlin Co.	1,389,000	12
34. David M. Grant & Partners	1,321,063	12
35. Noonan/Russo Communications	1,307,022	16
36. Diana M. Orban Assocs.	1,234,376	15
37. Trimedia/NYCOM	1,211,055	15
38. Cairns and Assocs.	1,148,492	20
39. Van Vechten & Assocs.	1,133,403	11
40. Alan Taylor Communications	1,081,046	17
41. Kovak Thomas Public Relations	1,008,850	12
42. Middleton & Picower	997,718	13
43. Jeff Blumenfeld & Assocs.	881,495	10
44. Padilla Speer Beardsley	851,800	7
45. The Kamber Group	619,333	7
46. Robert Wick Public Relations	494,842	5
47. Visibility Public Relations	390,952	4
48. Molino + Assocs.	256,524	3
49. E. Bruce Harrison Co.	205,269	3
50. Lapin East	158,750	4
51. Steve Davis PR	118,000	2

CHICAGO

Firm	1990 Fee Income	Empl.
1. Hill and Knowlton	$12,200,000	117
2. Burson-Marsteller	11,300,000	112
3. Golin/Harris Comms. of Shandwick	10,236,000	130
4. Edelman PR Worldwide	8,753,082	116
5. Financial Relations Board	7,029,533	85
6. Aaron D. Cushman and Assocs.	3,775,848	47
7. Robinson, Lake, Lerer & Montgomery including Bozell PR	3,300,000	30
8. Omnicom PR Network (Porter/Novelli)	2,693,377	35
9. Public Communications	2,454,202	25
10. Manning, Selvage & Lee	2,402,000	23
11. Dragonette	2,356,386	30
12. Selz, Seabolt & Assocs.	2,349,289	32
13. Gibbs & Soell	2,112,363	23
14. Ketchum Public Relations	1,700,000	38
15. Weiser Minkus Walek Comms.	1,686,512	16
16. Ogilvy PR (Ogilvy & Mather PR)	1,570,000	18
17. L.C. Williams & Assocs.	1,541,014	20
18. Burrell Public Relations	1,540,000	17
19. Ruder Finn	1,262,000	20
20. Cohn & Wolfe	1,181,000	11
21. Media Strategy	681,815	10
22. Kendrick Communications	429,326	7
23. Fleishman-Hillard	409,000	8
24. DeFrancesco/Goodfriend PR	408,493	4
25. Investor Relations Co.	403,848	7
26. McKinney Public Relations	332,707	6
27. Trimedia	312,250	5

WASHINGTON, D.C.

Firm	1990 Fee Income	Empl.
1. Hill and Knowlton	$38,000,000	279
2. Burson-Marsteller	15,000,000	139
3. Powell, Adams & Rinehart of Ogilvy PR Group	9,113,000	88
4. Fleishman-Hillard	7,425,000	87
5. The Kamber Group	6,802,796	93
6. Porter/Novelli of Omnicom	6,237,920	55
7. E. Bruce Harrison Co.	4,623,484	38
8. Ketchum Public Relations	4,400,000	46
9. Robinson, Lake, Lerer & Montgomery including Bozell PR	4,300,000	30
10. Edelman PR Worldwide	3,572,711	25
11. Earle Palmer Brown/Madison Group	3,108,989	31
12. Smith & Harroff	2,006,210	12
13. Hager Sharp	1,701,701	19
14. Manning, Selvage & Lee	1,644,000	15
15. Ruder Finn	1,355,650	15

LOS ANGELES

Firm	1990 Fee Income	Empl.
1. Rogers & Cowan of Shandwick	$9,497,000	94
2. Hill and Knowlton	7,100,000	70
3. Manning, Selvage & Lee	6,033,000	57
4. Stoorza Ziegaus Metzger (San Diego)	4,472,557	65
5. Fleishman-Hillard	4,012,000	87
6. Ketchum Public Relations	3,800,000	38
7. Burson-Marsteller	3,400,000	35
8. Nelson Communications	3,082,949	31
9. Cerrell Assocs.	2,674,271	29
10. Pacific West Comms. Group	2,655,652	28
11. Bob Thomas of Chiat/Day/Mojo	2,500,000	30
12. Rogers & Assocs.	2,150,179	25
13. Edelman PR Worldwide	2,013,526	19
14. Dennis Davidson Assocs.	2,058,774	29
15. Boonshaft-Lewis & Savitch	1,755,457	12
16. Casey & Sayre	1,690,135	13
17. GCI Group	1,667,000	13
18. Gelman & Gray	1,611,400	22
19. Vista Group	1,600,404	7
20. The Bohle Co.	1,297,193	9
21. Porter/Novelli of Omnicom PR	1,032,738	16
22. Capital Relations, Agoura Hills	1,012,621	11
23. Ruder Finn	941,020	11
24. Paine & Assocs. (Costa Mesa)	903,791	12
25. Ogilvy & Mather PR/West	886,000	7
26. Russ Reid Co.	840,898	3
27. Lapin/West	621,295	7
28. Financial Relations Board	500,000	4
29. The Londre Co.	317,041	5

CITY/REGIONAL RANKING OF FIRMS SUBMITTING DOCUMENTATION TO O'DWYER'S DIR. OF PR FIRMS

BOSTON

Firm	1990 Fee Income	Empl.
1. Cone Communications	4,228,784	46
2. Miller Communs. of Shandwick	3,432,000	21
3. Clarke & Co.	3,054,234	33
4. BMc Strategies	2,802,906	19
5. Hill and Knowlton	2,400,000	23
6. Brodeur & Partners	1,535,959	15
7. Schneider & Assocs.	879,353	8
8. Copithorne & Bellows	600,000	8

NEW JERSEY

Firm	1990 Fee Income	Empl.
1. Holt, Ross & Yulish, Edison	2,495,355	31
2. MWW Strategic Comms., River Edge	2,399,245	18
3. MCS (Mgmt. Comms. Svcs.), Summit.	1,397,159	14

PHILADELPHIA

Firm	1990 Fee Income	Empl.
1. Ketchum Public Relations	2,400,000	26
2. Earle Palmer Brown Public Relations	1,452,595	11
3. Golin/Harris Communications	1,600,000	21
4. McKinney Public Relations	781,964	12
5. Fleishman-Hillard	770,000	13

PITTSBURGH

Firm	1990 Fee Income	Empl.
1. Ketchum Public Relations	4,300,000	46
2. Hill and Knowlton	2,500,000	14
3. Burson-Marsteller	2,200,000	26
4. Skutski & Assocs.	1,393,912	17

ATLANTA

Firm	1990 Fee Income	Empl.
1. Cohn & Wolfe	5,138,000	49
2. Hill and Knowlton	3,200,000	32
3. Manning, Selvage & Lee	2,844,000	30
4. Ketchum Public Relations	2,000,000	28
5. Fleishman-Hillard	894,000	14
6. Ogilvy & Mather Public Relations	438,000	4

SOUTHEAST

Firm	1990 Fee Income	Empl.
1. Dye, Van Mol & Lawrence, Nashville	3,060,571	56
2. Charles Ryan Assocs., Charleston	2,526,767	39
3. Hank Meyer Assocs., Miami	2,314,546	26
4. Burson-Marsteller, Miami	1,800,000	23
5. Wenz-Neely of Shandwick, Louisville	1,591,600	13
6. Price-McNabb, Asheville, N.C.	1,347,350	12
7. Bruce Rubin Assocs., Miami	1,020,221	13
8. Hill and Knowlton, Tampa	1,000,000	11
9. Public Communications, Tampa	811,332	12
10. Gibbs & Soell, Raleigh, N.C.	760,094	8
11. Earle Palmer Brown, Richmond, Va.	689,916	9
12. Sanchez & Levitan, Miami	633,029	12
13. Bennett & Co., Miami Beach	461,113	8

OHIO

Firm	1990 Fee Income	Empl.
1. Dix & Eaton, Cleveland	4,800,731	47
2. Edward Howard & Co., Cleveland	3,452,700	37
3. Watt, Roop & Co., Cleveland	2,327,850	27
4. Funk/Luetke, Toledo	1,478,052	22
5. Proconsul Div. of Jayme Org., Cleve.	1,457,523	15
6. McKinney Public Relations, Cleve.	644,176	9
7. Robert Carter & Assocs., Cleveland	310,000	7

DETROIT

Firm	1990 Fee Income	Empl.
1. Casey Comms. Mgmt. of Shandwick	3,455,000	18
2. Manning, Selvage & Lee	862,000	14

MIDWEST CITIES

Firm	1990 Fee Income	Empl.
1. Mona, Meyer & McGrath of Shandwick, Minneapolis	6,454,500	57
2. Padilla Speer Beardsley, Minneapolis	3,629,800	42
3. Bader Rutter & Assocs., Milwaukee	3,325,099	40
4. Fleishman-Hillard, Kansas City, Mo.	3,114,000	33
5. CMF&Z, Cedar Rapids, Iowa	2,640,717	31
6. Morgan & Myers, Milwaukee	2,075,647	37
7. The Boasberg Co., Kansas City, Mo.	1,708,584	24
8. Communications Concepts Unltd., Racine, Wis.	1,571,038	15
9. Spectrum Comms., Kansas City, Mo.	582,975	10

ST. LOUIS

Firm	1990 Fee Income	Empl.
1. Fleishman-Hillard	19,642,000	225
2. Hill and Knowlton	2,500,000	30
3. Dorf & Stanton of Shandwick	1,725,500	22
4. Edelman Public Relations Worldwide	968,708	11
5. Tretter-Gorman	868,407	11

DALLAS

Firm	1990 Fee Income	Empl.
1. Tracy-Locke PR of Omnicom	1,877,800	18
2. Bloom Public Relations	1,503,000	16
3. E. Bruce Harrison Co.	824,999	8
4. Hill and Knowlton	700,000	10
5. Anderson Fischel Thompson div. of J.Walter Thompson	647,326	10
6. Edelman Public Relations Worldwide	641,466	5
7. Meltzer & Martin	529,281	7

HOUSTON

Firm	1990 Fee Income	Empl.
1. Edelman Public Relations Worldwide	1,816,974	12
2. Hill and Knowlton	1,000,000	10
3. Gibbs & Soell	495,114	4

WESTERN CITIES

Firm	1990 Fee Income	Empl.
1. The Rockey Co., Seattle	4,255,381	56
2. Elgin Syferd of Omnicom, Seattle	1,808,478	20
3. Stoorza, Ziegaus & Metzger, Sacramento	1,759,460	13
4. Carl Thompson & Assocs., Boulder, Colo.	1,211,003	26
5. Nelson Communications, Phoenix	1,071,464	13

SAN FRANCISCO

Firm	1990 Fee Income	Empl.
1. Ketchum Public Relations	6,400,000	58
2. Hi-Tech PR of Shandwick	4,862,000	27
3. Burson-Marsteller	2,000,000	20
4. Hill and Knowlton	2,000,000	11
5. Edelman Public Relations Worldwide	1,720,129	17
6. Porter/Novelli of Omnicom	1,329,024	20
7. Solem Assocs.	1,314,639	17
8. Copithorne & Bellows	1,100,000	15
9. Ogilvy & Mather PR	777,000	11
10. Cohn & Wolfe	365,000	3
11. Financial Relations Board	100,000	3

SILICON VALLEY

Firm	1990 Fee Income	Empl.
1. Cunningham Comms., Santa Clara	3,475,945	34
2. Franson, Hagerty & Assocs.	2,423,000	20
3. PRx, San Jose	2,375,109	30
4. Ketchum PR, Sunnyvale	2,100,000	25
5. Hill and Knowlton, Santa Clara	2,000,000	17
6. Gibbs & Soell, Carmel	943,296	
7. Thomas Asocs., Menlo Park	711,163	7
8. Tycer Fultz Bellack, Palo Alto	506,000	6

FEE INCOME ACCORDING TO AREAS OF SPECIALIZATION
(Headquarters city is New York unless otherwise indicated)

AGRICULTURE
1. Gibbs & Soell 3,461,000
2. Bader Rutter & Assocs.,
   Brookfield, Wis. 2,651,224
3. Shandwick 2,040,000
4. Morgan & Myers, Milw. ... 1,588,741
5. CMF&Z, Cedar Rapids, Ia.. 1,463,968

BEAUTY/FASHION
1. Hill and Knowlton 10,000,000
2. Burson-Marsteller 3,000,000
3. Porter/Novelli (Omnicom) . 2,184,824
4. DeVries PR 1,980,659
5. Manning, Selvage & Lee.. 1,500,000
6. Ayer Public Relations ... 1,482,359
7. Cairns & Assocs. 1,148,492
8. Cone Comms., Boston .. 682,374
9. Patrice Tanaka & Co. 520,400
10. Ruder Finn 500,000
11. Edelman PR Worldwide . 297,000
12. Tretter-Gorman, St. Louis. 3,750

ENTERTAINMENT/CULTURAL
1. Shandwick 7,090,000
2. Burson-Marsteller 2,000,000
3. Hill and Knowlton 1,000,000
4. Manning, Selvage & Lee . 1,000,000
5. Edelman PR Worldwide . 891,000
6. Cohn & Wolfe, Atlanta .. 769,000
7. Ruder Finn 500,000
8. Cone Comms., Boston .. 401,500
9. Aaron D. Cushman, Chi.. 345,000
10. Lapin East/West, LA and NY. 209,512
11. GCI Group 96,000

ENVIRONMENTAL
1. Hill and Knowlton 17,000,000
2. Burson-Marsteller 15,000,000
3. Ketchum Public Relations . 9,600,000
4. Shandwick 6,299,000
5. E. Bruce Harrison Co.,DC.. 3,900,000
6. Edelman PR Worldwide . 3,240,000
7. Ruder Finn 3,000,000
8. BMc Strategies, Lexington,
   Mass. 2,571,637
9. Pacific/West Comms.,L.A.. 2,533,036
10. Manning, Selvage & Lee.. 2,000,000
11. Holt, Ross & Yulish, Edison,
   N.J. 1,512,000
12. MMW/Strategic Comms.,
   River Edge, N.J. 1,100,000
13. Porter/Novelli (Omnicom) 1,008,418
14. Cohn & Wolfe, Atlanta .. 519,000
15. Cone Comms., Boston .. 126,000
16. GCI Group 79,900
17. Tretter-Gorman, St. Louis. 74,339
18. Morgan & Myers, Milw. .. 57,809

FINANCIAL PR/INVESTOR RELS.
1. Hill and Knowlton 44,000,000
2. Ogilvy Adams & Rinehart
   Network 19,740,000
3. Burson-Marsteller 17,000,000
4. Financial Relations Board,
   Chicago 9,540,626
5. Corporate Communs. ... 8,428,124
6. Shandwick 6,671,000
7. Dewe Rogerson 4,444,000

8. Ruder Finn 4,000,000
9. Manning, Selvage & Lee . 4,000,000
10. Edelman PR Worldwide . 3,670,000
11. Morgen-Walke 3,638,767
12. Ketchum Public Rels. 2,100,000
13. GCI Group 1,649,300
14. Makovsky & Co. 1,500,000
15. Trimedia 1,332,460
16. KCS&A Public Relations . 1,330,000
17. Porter/Novelli (Omnicom). 1,267,416
18. Carl Thompson & Assocs.,
   Boulder, Colo. 1,211,003
19. Selz, Seabolt & Assocs.,
   Chicago 409,906
20. Investor Relations Co., Chi.. 403,848

FOODS & BEVERAGES
1. Hill and Knowlton 29,000,000
2. Burson-Marsteller 20,000,000
3. Shandwick 12,873,000
4. Ketchum Public Relations 9,400,000
5. Edelman PR Worldwide . 7,004,000
6. Porter/Novelli of Omnicom. 3,037,062
7. Manning, Selvage & Lee . 3,000,000
8. Cohn & Wolfe, Atlanta ... 2,025,000
9. Ruder Finn 1,500,000
10. Aaron D. Cushman, Chi. . 1,000,000
11. Cone Comms., Boston .. 857,783
12. GCI Group 656,200
13. Selz, Seabolt & Assocs.,
   Chicago 393,523
14. Morgan & Myers, Milw. .. 377,467
15. Londre Co., Los Angeles . 317,041
16. DeVries Public Relations . 302,000
17. Patrice Tanaka & Co. 293,500
18. Kovak-Thomas PR 154,833
19. MWW/Strategic Comms.,
   River Edge, N.J. 118,000
20. Tretter-Gorman, St. Louis. 16,500

HEALTHCARE
1. Burson-Marsteller 38,000,000
2. Hill and Knowlton 18,000,000
3. Ruder Finn 8,500,000
4. Porter/Novelli (Omnicom). 7,016,630
5. Manning, Selvage & Lee . 7,000,000
6. Ketchum Public Relations. 6,500,000
7. Edelman PR Worldwide . 6,466,000
8. Shandwick 4,103,000
9. Cohn & Wolfe, Atlanta .. 2,611,000
10. Gross Townsend Frank
   Hoffman 2,500,000
11. Wang Associates 2,036,064
12. Public Comms., Chicago. 1,740,565
13. Lobsenz-Stevens 1,481,500
14. MCS. (Mgmt. Comms. Svcs.).
   Summit, N.J. 1,397,159
15. Noonan/Russo Comms. . 1,307,022
16. Cone Comms., Boston .. 1,198,007
17. Van Vechten & Assocs. .. 904,609
18. Kovak-Thomas PR 565,385
19. KCS&A Public Relations . 525,000
20. Aaron D. Cushman, Chi.. 495,000
21. Robert Carter & Assocs.,
   Cleveland 310,000
22. Makovsky & Co. 225,000
23. Patrice Tanaka & Co. 150,000
24. MWW/Strategic Comms.,
   River Edge, N.J. 116,000
25. Tretter-Gorman, St. Louis . 33,021

HIGH-TECH
1. Hill and Knowlton 23,000,000
2. Shandwick 17,347,000
3. Burson-Marsteller 10,000,000
4. Ketchum Public Relations. 6,500,000
5. Manning, Selvage & Lee . 5,500,000
6. Cunningham Comms.,
   Santa Clara 3,475,945
7. Edelman PR Worldwide 3,354,000
8. Ruder Finn 2,500,000
9. Franson, Hagerty & Assocs.,
   San Jose 2,423,000
10. PRx, San Jose 2,375,109
11. Copithorne & Bellows, San
   Francisco 1,678,154
12. Makovsky & Co. 1,400,000
13. GCI Group 1,305,600
14. Porter/Novelli, New York, and Tycer-
   Fultz-Bellack, Palo Alto
   (Omnicom) 824,484
15. Cohn & Wolfe, Atlanta .. 296,000
16. DeVries Public Relations . 148,282
17. Tretter-Gorman, St. Louis. 99,965
18. Morgan & Myers, Milw. .. 51,630
19. BMc Strategies, Lexington,
   Mass. 38,660

SPORTS
1. Burson-Marsteller 8,000,000
2. Hill and Knowlton 3,000,000
3. Edelman PR Worldwide . 2,496,000
4. Cohn & Wolfe, Atlanta ... 2,357,000
5. Manning, Selvage & Lee . 1,500,000
6. Alan Taylor Comms. 1,081,046
7. Ruder Finn 600,000
8. Lapin East/West 567,000
9. Cone Comms., Boston .. 506,152
10. Selz, Seabolt & Assocs.,
   Chicago 337,052
11. Jeff Blumenfeld and Assocs. 291,098
12. Public Comms., Chicago. 204,564
13. Davis Public Relations .. 72,000
14. Tretter-Gorman, St. Louis. 44,400

TRAVEL
1. Hill and Knowlton 16,000,000
2. Shandwick 5,345,000
3. GCI Group 3,073,000
4. Manning, Selvage & Lee . 2,500,000
5. M. Silver Assocs. 2,430,006
6. Burson-Marsteller 2,000,000
7. Lou Hammond & Assocs. 1,854,000
8. Edelman PR Worldwide . 1,796,000
9. Porter/Novelli (Omnicom). 1,423,780
10. Diana M. Orban Assocs. . 1,234,376
11. Cohn & Wolfe, Atlanta .. 854,000
12. Ruder Finn 600,000
13. Aaron D. Cushman and Assocs.,
   Chicago 510,000
14. Patrice Tanaka & Co. 509,400
15. Public Comms., Chicago . 268,750
16. MWW Strategic Comms.,
   River Edge, N.J. 140,000
17. DeVries Public Relations 73,250
18. Tretter-Gorman, St. Louis. 21,900

- **Public Relations Society of America (PRSA),** 33 Irving Place, New York, 10003, (212) 995-2230, publishes descriptions of the winning programs in its annual Silver Anvil Awards. Many of the winning programs are agency programs.

- **International Association of Business Communicators (IABC),** One Hallidie Plaza, Suite 600, San Francisco, CA, 94102, publishes summaries of its annual Gold Quill Award winners.

Other Important Factors

You may have received letters, calls, or personal solicitations from PR firms when you weren't in the market. Firms that have indicated in the past that they are interested in your business deserve to be considered in the initial round.

Personal exposure and personal recommendation play a key role in agency selection. Client executives may know local public relations executives on a first-name basis from working with them in the business community. Other valuable sources of information are business friends and acquaintances. A good way to start getting a line on PR firms is by talking to and networking with peers in other companies and fellow members of business and civic groups.

Trade sources, including trade association staff and members can be particularly valuable. Many a PR firm has been hired by a company belonging to a trade group because of its work for and knowledge of the industry represented by the association.

Those PR firms that practice for themselves what they preach to clients, i.e. good agency PR, are likely to get attention from clients who read business and trade publications or scan computerized data bases for published articles by or about PR firms. Many PR firms make it their business to write articles and give, publicize, and distribute speeches. They make local news by commenting on issues, growing their business, getting new accounts, and promoting their executives. The cumulative effect is to keep their name in the news.

This not only gives the agency visibility in the business community but demonstrates their ability to do the same for their clients.

Look also to PR firms that participate in civic and community affairs, fund raising campaigns, and business executive clubs and that play an active leadership role in their own field by participating in professional societies like PRSA and IABC.

Some PR firms have organized direct mail programs targeted to prospective clients and potential recommenders with newsletters, client success stories, speeches, articles, and PR materials. Others emphasize recognition by their peers through merchandising awards they have won in industry competitions sponsored by the Public Relations Society of America, the International Association of Business Communicators, and local publicity and ad clubs.

Some PR firms advertise in O'Dwyer's directories, in PR trade publications, and in other business and trade publications and achieve positive local exposure by running ads in the programs of philanthropic or cultural events attended by the city's movers and shakers. Other public relations devices used by PR firms include underwriting public radio programming and public television fund-raising efforts.

The Media as a Source

If your primary interest in retaining a PR firm is to obtain publicity, the media can be a valuable source. A good place to start is with the local media. Call local newspaper, television, and radio reporters and ask them which firms provide them with accurate information, respond promptly to their queries, and provide them with good story leads.

Jack O'Dwyer says, "Ask what people are currently doing good work. Find out who reporters trust, who is in day-to-day contact with the reporters and who are experts in their industry. Talk to four or five reporters for balance in case one of them is partial to a particular PR firm."[2]

If you are interested in coverage in business media, you would do well to talk to financial editors of the the major daily newspapers and editors of business magazines. They deal on a continuing basis with PR firms with major corporate clients and are in a position to know which ones provide them with useful material and access to client top management. The same is true down the line. A food editor knows who to work with on a feature story and who provides reliable information about products and nutrition.

A valuable source for information about PR firms serving a particular industry are the editors of the trade books serving that industry. They personally know and work closely with the PR people representing the trade associations and companies with effective PR programs. If your account is going to be in the investor relations area, you can talk to financial analysts who cover the industry, evaluate the players, and are often quoted in the business press. Corporate members of the National Investor Relations Institute (NIRI) are another good source.

Importance of Recommendations

Corporate PR chiefs of Fortune 500 companies surveyed by PR consultant Alfred Geduldig cited references as the most important reason for including an agency on the long list.

A respondent to J.R. O'Dwyer's Survey of Corporate Attitudes Toward Outside PR Counsel advises clients using PR firms for the first time to "talk to former clients as well as current clients. Always take a good look at their press releases. Be specific as to what you expect the PR firm to accomplish and in what time period. Ask the press how they perceive the PR firm."[3]

Fraser Seitel, senior vice-president and director of Public Affairs, Chase Manhattan Bank, New York, and author of *The Practice of Public Relations*, emphasizes the importance of checking out references even of the larger, well known firms. In soliciting references, he recommends asking former clients specific questions. For example:

- What was the nature of the assignment you had the consultant work on?

- Was it finished on time, on budget, with a pleasant attitude?

- Are you still using what was produced?

- How would you suggest I use this consultant and agency staff?

He believes that references can be invaluable not only in determining the worth of a particular consultant but also in structuring your specific assignment.[4]

Absence of Conflict

While all respondents to the Geduldig survey said they would not pick a firm where direct conflict was involved, clients value experience in their particular field. He concludes that "the ideal situation is where the firm has just quit a major competitor ten minutes before presenting."

Don't assume that your information is up to date when it comes to client conflicts. The firm may no longer be serving your competitor as listed in last year's O'Dwyer's Directory. They may be free and, in fact, a prime candidate for your business based on their experience in your field. Nor can you assume that the firm's relationship with its competitive client is a happy one. Circumstances may exist where the agency would give up their client for your account.

How Long Should the Long List Be?

On the basis of recommendations, past experience, and your research of PR, community, business, trade, and media sources, you should now be ready to draw up the long list. You will want to contact a manageable number of firms. What is a manageable number? There is no all-purpose answer, although consultant Robert Ferrante suggests that the initial long list contain "no more than twenty, but ideally a dozen" firms. It depends in part on how much time you are willing to invest in screening PR firms, how many you are prepared to visit, and how willing you are to brief a number of outsiders about your company's public relations problems.

Another consideration is the effect of the size of the list on the firms you contact. Participating in a competitive agency selection situation is a very time consuming business, and while most agencies welcome the opportunity, they may be reluctant to play if they feel the odds are stacked against them. The agency that learns that more than 20 agencies are on the long list may treat this as a challenge and go for broke. On the other hand, they may believe that they don't stand a chance against formidable opponents with more appropriate credentials and decline to participate. A prime example are the RFPs (request for proposal) issued by government agencies and state commissions which by law must issue a general request for proposal to all interested firms. The U.S. Army and the Florida Citrus Commission have found few agencies willing to put forth the effort to solicit their advertising accounts when it is widely felt that the client is happy with the current agency, that an agency change would be disruptive and expensive, and that they are going through the motions as prescribed by law.

Before finalizing the long list, you will probably want to tell your advertising agency about the search for a PR firm. They may or may not be interested in the PR assignment. After talking to them, you may determine that their PR services are not comparable to those offered by the PR firms on your list. On the other hand, if you think they are qualified and interested, you may want to add them to the list. In this case, they and the other competing PR firms must be specifically assured that the ad agency has no inside track on the PR business.

References

1. O'Dwyer, "How to Hire and Get the Most from Outside PR Counsel," 141.

2. Ibid., 140.

3. "Survey Shock: PR Firms Don't Give Money's Worth," *O'Dwyer's PR Services Report* (July 1991), 10.

4. Fraser P. Seitel, "How to Hire a PR Firm," *O'Dwyer's Directory of Public Relations Firms 1991*, (New York: J.R. O'Dwyer Co., 1991), A 145.

CHAPTER 4

Contacting PR Firms

It is now time to begin the formal process of contacting PR firms. Or is it? Sometimes the need for a PR firm is perceived and the process initiated before the necessary approvals have been received from management.

Counselor James Strenski, chairman of Public Communications, Inc., says there are two factors that clients must consider before they begin to contact PR firms. First the company "should be sure it really wants to buy" before it solicits proposals. He points out that too often organizations waste a great deal of their time, as well as that of public relations firms, when they solicit several proposals without convincing their own management that public relations counsel is really needed.

The second factor cited by Strenski is to understand that "public relations counselors sell communications talent in increments of time and their ability to serve you well is directly related to how effectively they use their time and how efficiently and promptly the input resources of your company are available to them."[1] In other words, you should go into an agency search with a realistic idea of the cost of paying the firm for its time and expending the staff time necessary to manage the agency's work.

Your public relations counterparts in other client companies and the PR firms themselves will be able to give you an idea of the rates charged by PR firms for their time. Of course, every PR program differs in terms of required time involvement but a basic knowledge of how PR firms charge for their time will tell you if your budget is in the ballpark.

Making Contact

When you have determined that management is committed to fund an agency PR program, you should be ready to send a questionnaire to the long list of PR firms you have selected. The purpose of the questionnaire is not only to identify viable candidates for the account but to begin the process of screening and eliminating unsuitable PR firms before spending your time and resources meeting with them.

Many clients initiate contact personally by telephoning the presidents of the PR firms on their long list to determine if they are interested and if they have obvious client conflicts that disqualify them. Since the public relations firm will be a business partner to the client, it will be privy to sensitive and highly confidential information. The client must be assured that this information cannot fall into the hands of its competitors. The question of client conflict is much discussed in both advertising and public relations circles. Some clients insist that their agencies not work for any company with which it competes in any product line. Others restrict agencies only in product specific categories. Agencies largely believe that conflicts of interest exist primarily in the eyes of the client. They believe they should be able to represent more than one company in the same industry if the accounts are managed from different offices or special precautionary measures are taken to "build a Chinese Wall" between the account teams assigned to each client.

The availability of the agency head and the initial response to your "cold call" may provide some valuable clues about the firm's service orientation and enthusiasm about the opportunity of working with you.

Whether or not initial personal contact is made by phone, a formal follow-up should be confirmed in writing. Each agency should be sent a letter explaining the search and officially notifying them that their firm is being considered. This agency should be asked to confirm their interest in the account. The answer is not always an automatic "yes." The agency may have a competitive account. It may not want an account the size of the one being offered. The firm may feel the account is too small or, in some cases, too large for them to handle. The agency may decline if it feels it isn't able to offer the specific services, offices, or specialized skills outlined in the letter or that it would otherwise have a poor chance to win the account in a competition with more qualified firms.

The transmittal letter should:

- describe the specific public relations assignment (account) for which the client is seeking a PR firm
- provide a basic description of the company's public relations needs
- describe the questionnaire and ask that it be completed and returned by a specified date
- advise that the next step in the selection process will be to schedule an informal visit with the agency to personally meet with the agency heads and become fully acquainted with its people and capabilities
- advise the agency that it is one of a number of agencies being contacted

The letter might also set public relations budget parameters. In their book *What Happens in Public Relations*, Gerald Voros and Paul Alvarez of Ketchum Communications state:

> It is reasonable to assume that the manager will be able to roughly estimate the amount of money he expects to spend on outside services, including out-of-pocket expenses. This information should be supplied to agencies so they can judge the importance of the potential client and the amount of agency resources to be devoted to the client if the agency gets the assignment.[2]

Stating the budget parameters at the outset will help the recipient agency determine if the account is too small to handle profitably, if it is realistically too large to handle without major staff or office expansion, and if it is of marginal or major interest. Knowing this in advance will save time for both the agency completing the questionnaire and the client in screening the responses.

Avoiding the RFP Syndrome

While you may not wish to reveal the exact number of agencies you are initially contacting, you should indicate that it is a select group. By doing this, you can distinguish your solicitation from the RFPs (request for proposal) issued by some organizations. The practice of contacting all firms on a comprehensive list or opening the solicitation to anyone who wants to participate was established by governmental bodies to give the appearance of fairness and avoid the appearance of favoritism. In fact, some RFPs even state that if the recipient firm is not interested in participating, it would be appreciated if they would pass the REP along to other qualified firms. Another reason that governmental bodies and some other organizations issue RFPs is that they believe they will get the best price for the job.

The RFP approach is discouraged for a number of reasons. Many PR firms refuse to respond to RFPs on principle. They are not willing to spend hours and days completing an elaborate questionnaire if they know they will be competing with the entire PR world for the account and that, therefore, the chances of their getting the account are slim to none. Under these circumstances, they may not want to reveal proprietary information about their firm, including its pricing structure. In order to provide this information, they may want the client to identify the firm as one of a select group of viable candidates for the business.

Most PR firms can be expected to react negatively to the depersonalization of a process which has as its desired outcome the establishment of an essentially personal client-agency relationship. As firms that have responded to RFPs well know, not only is the business of completing questionnaires very time-consuming, but the next step may be a "cattle call" briefing of all interested firms. While the client may do this to save time, PR firms who are willing to proceed to the next step in the selection process believe they deserve an opportunity to meet individually with the client. This enables them to begin establishing personal rapport with the client and to follow a line of questioning without revealing the direction of their thinking to a room full of competitors.

Finally, the call for RFPs sends a signal that the client sees public relations firms as vendors rather than business partners and does not differentiate between the quality of work and the price paid for it.

Clients considering sending an RFP should recognize these objections and know that many of the best qualified candidates will eliminate themselves. There is a real chance that the list of interested firms will be limited to those that need the business, have time on their hands to go through the process, and have no objection to working as a low-cost supplier of public relations services.

The Agency Questionnaire

The questionnaire should be designed to eliminate firms with a direct conflict or insufficient experience in a desired area of specialization. It should include certain basic information:

1. Headquarters
2. Agency size
3. Ownership/parent
4. List of key agency officers
5. Reach—local, regional, national, international
6. Location of offices/affiliates
7. Agency size (current net fee income)
8. Agency income (past five years)
9. Size per office: U.S. and world-wide

10. Number of employees (total and per office)

11. Public Relations services offered:
    media relations
    public affairs
    employee relations
    government relations/lobbying
    marketing public relations/product publicity
    investor relations
    crisis communications

12. Other specialized areas of practice

13. Percent of total practice represented by each

14. List of current clients; length of time with agency; current assignments for each

15. Any client you think might be a potential conflict

16. Research capability (facilities, staff, use of data bases, primary research)

17. Other in-house services (design, desktop publishing, broadcast production, etc.)

18. Statement of agency philosophy

19. Experience in our field

20. Parallel experience to our needs

21. Method of agency compensation

Some clients may want to obtain more detailed information. For example, their questionnaire may ask for more detailed information on how the PR firm is compensated for its services (i.e., monthly retainer fee, project fee, billing for actual staff time or on an hourly or per diem basis or a formula of time against fee). Does the agency add a mark-up for expenses or purchases? Does it place a value-added charge on counsel or link compensation to achievement of pre-determined goals? Most big PR firms have followed the lead of law, consulting, and other professional service firms and are charging by the hour.

Clients may also want to request information about:

- new accounts, last 12 months
- accounts lost, last 12 months
- largest account; percent of agency/office income
- other large accounts that account for more than 20 percent of income
- distribution of agency business by size of client (as percent of total net fee income)
- the agency's financial condition
- recruitment and training programs
- staff turnover
- organization chart
- participation in accounts by top management
- public relations process
- reporting procedure
- PRSA/IABC membership
- participation in PRSA Counselors Academy
- accreditation of agency executives
- agency history
- references; contacts at agency clients

In addition to the completed questionnaire, the client may request agency brochures, promotional material, and samples of agency work. Since the information requested is readily available, the agency should be asked to respond within ten days of receipt. The transmittal letter should indicate the specific date by which the completed questionnaire must be returned. It should also discourage calls and questions from agencies at this early stage in the solicitation process. The information requested on a well written questionnaire should be self-explanatory. However, there may be circumstances when an agency will have a legitimate need to contact the client. For example, to determine whether the soliciting client considers an existing client of the PR firm to be a conflict.

Differences between PR and Advertising Questionnaires

One common mistake made by clients inexperienced in selecting PR firms is to try to adapt the questionnaire they use when screening advertising agencies. While there are similarities in the relationship clients have with their PR and advertising firms, and while the PR assignment may also be marketing-related, there are basic differences which should be recognized. The client that sends an unedited advertising-type questionnaire to a PR firm reveals not only its lack of knowledge about PR firms but also about the public relations function.

The PR firm receiving such a questionnaire faces a dilemma. It can pretend to answer the questions, no matter how unsuitable to public relations, or it can point out to the client that the questions are inappropriate—a less-than-positive way to begin a relationship with a potential new client.

For example, the advertising-derived questionnaire typically includes questions about "billings." This advertising term refers to the cost of broadcast time and print space which the agency buys on behalf of the client to run advertising. With the exception of issue advocacy, crisis management, or mergers and acquisition campaigns where advertising is used as a public relations tactic, PR firms do not normally buy time and space so the question is not applicable. Since the purpose of the question is to determine agency size, the PR firm will either have to substitute its net fee income or apply a 6.7 multiplier to equate its income with advertising "billings."

Another impossible-to-equate question that often appears on the questionnaires of the PR-uninformed company relates to billings per media. Since PR firms do not normally buy time on radio or television, space in newspapers or magazines, or advertising in any other commissionable "non traditional media," the question can't be answered. The polite PR firm may try to estimate how much "free time and space" it may be able to gain in various media through its publicity efforts. This will in all likelihood be no more than a wild guess, since PR firms have no reason to total the results of unlike media relations programs for unlike clients.

Other advertising type questions to avoid concern media planning and media buying. While some PR firms have a department called a media department, its name is misleading and its function entirely different from the advertising agency's media department which crunches numbers, recommends media plans based on cost efficiencies, and negotiates media buys. The PR media department is really a media relations department which manages the relationship between the company and the editorial side of the media. It both responds to and initiates contact with the media.

There is greater similarity between the research function of advertising and PR firms but here, too, there are significant differences. One of the principal functions of the advertising research department is to test the effectiveness of ads and commercials. While public relations research can be used to test messages, the headlines and specific copy used by the media to communicate these messages are the province of editors and reporters, not public relations writers. PR can suggest copy through news releases but cannot control the words that ultimately appear in the media. Public relations research is more likely to be concerned with content analysis, public opinion, and tracking attitude change.

Handling the Questionnaires

The search committee chairperson should be able to assemble the completed questionnaires within a week of the deadline. A complete package of questionnaires should then be provided to all committee members with a cover memorandum listing the agencies that responded and any that disqualified themselves or were clearly disqualified under the ground rules of the search. The chairperson might also want to raise other pertinent questions.

On the basis of the questionnaire, each member of the committee will be asked to rate the agencies in order, from those they believe are most qualified to those that are least qualified for the assignment at hand.

The chairperson should tabulate the ratings and call a committee meeting to review the results. There may be a clear consensus on the qualification of some agencies and questions to be answered or differences of opinion to be resolved on others. This meeting offers committee members the opportunity to provide input not specifically related to the questionnaire. For example, they may have personal experience with one or more of the agencies or want to call the committee's attention to references from trusted industry sources. As a result of the meeting, the committee may want to expand or narrow the number of agencies on the short list.

References

1. James B. Strenski, "Ten Criteria for Selecting Public Relations Counsel," *Public Relations Journal* (July 1985), 11.

2. Gerald Voros and Paul Alvarez, *What Happens in Public Relations*, (AMACOM, 1981) Ann Arbor, MI, 216.

CHAPTER 5

The Get-Acquainted Meeting

The long list should now be narrowed to a short list of four to six viable contenders. You must notify both the winners and the losers immediately and simultaneously. You will want to contact those that have been eliminated and thank them for their efforts in your behalf. In turn, you should be prepared to answer, in a general way, questions on why they were dropped.

It is also time to deliver the good news to the firms that have survived the cut and alert them to the next step of the selection process, a face-to-face, get-acquainted meeting.

The purpose of this meeting is to enable you to get a feel for the agency and its people. It also gives you the opportunity to ask questions raised by the agency's response to your questionnaire and to determine the extent of the agency's interest in your account.

Advantages of Meeting at the Agency

During the selection process, you will probably want to meet the agencies on the short list at least once in their offices and once in yours. There are definite advantages to meeting the firm initially on its own home ground. You should plan to make time to tour the agency to get a feel for its pace and workstyle. The advantage of meeting at the agency is the additional opportunity to size up the firm on its own turf where it has greater control of the amenities and the equipment.

PR counselor Bradley Lynch told Jack O'Dwyer "You can judge the size and strength of an agency best by a visit. Bad things to look for are offices that are empty, outdated clippings on the walls, secretaries who read magazines. Pluses you may find are fast-clicking typewriters, the frequent jangle of incoming phone calls, some clutter—that's often the badge of busy, creative people. Look at the back-up facilities. Is there a modern copying machine? You'll need these to get out fast-breaking news stories. Ask about the kinds of mailing lists the agency uses and how they keep them up-to-date. Is there a cable address for the firm? This is important if you want them to work in international PR."[1] Substitute computers for typewriters, add fax machines, data base retrieval hardware, voice mail and personal answering machines and you have the necessary accoutrements of the PR office of the 90s.

Veteran consultants stress the importance of first impressions and believe a firm is likely to "be itself" at home. Al Croft says the first encounter between firm and prospect is critical, perhaps even more critical than corporate executives and firm managers may recognize. He points out that impressions made during this visit will weigh heavily in the selection process and may even overcome the organized frenzy of formal presentations. In many instances the first meeting will determine whether the agency will be invited to make a final presentation. Croft says the initial meeting or briefing is an opportunity for the public relations firm to dig into the client's background and needs, and establish direction for the PR presentation. It is an opportunity for the prospect "to preview of firm's experience, eagerness, and intuitiveness in an unfettered, unstructured atmosphere."[2]

Meeting on Your Turf

If it is impossible for the selection committee to block out the necessary time for on-site visits during this initial round, each of the PR agencies should be invited to your offices. In either case, no more than two agencies a day should be seen. Each agency should be asked to make a capabilities presentation. Typically this is a 90-minute to two-hour meeting, including discussion. Your letter notifying them that they have been selected for the next round should specify the content of the presentation to make certain that all agencies are responding to a clear statement of your expectations within the context of their own individuality. They should be asked to discuss their public relations and business philosophy, resources, strategic approach, experience, and results with clients who have had public relations problems and needs similar to yours. This usually involves exposition of relevant client case histories.

Robert Ferrante believes that the first meeting should be devoted to testing the "chemistry" or compatibility of the firm's style and culture and evaluating its professionalism as reflected in the presentation of its credentials by senior people. He recommends that the firm be advised to devote no more than half of the allotted time of the meeting to presenting its credentials. The other half should be devoted to an exchange of questions and information relating to the client's needs.

In his book *Getting the Best from Your Ad Agency*, advertising executive Joe Marconi describes the credentials meeting as "a virtual bringing-to-life of the listing directory and questionnaire response." He suggests that the client present a memo to the agency stating all the things they need to know to make an intelligent presentation to the client firm:

1. Note the problems, questions, and concerns you wish the agency to address in its presentation.

2. Identify who will represent the client and request the names and functions of those who will be present for the agency. Specifically ask that the persons who will be working day-to-day on the account be present.

3. Describe any constraints the agency must work under, such as corporate (or parent company) identity standards.

4. Offer specific information regarding budget limits, prior commitments of the budget, any other relationships (ad agency consultants, research firm, etc.), and any research that might either be available or considered in the presentation.

5. Be specific about deadlines for agency selection.

Marconi says that at this meeting the client and prospective agency have an opportunity to size up one another. He concludes: "Whether or not you believe in the value of first impressions or 'gut feelings,' don't underestimate the value of the unsaid words or the 'vibrations'."[3]

Meeting Agenda

The agency will be in a better position to address your needs if you open the meeting with a discussion of the search process and the nature of the assignment. One of the best organized screening meetings I participated in as an agency head was conducted by a management consulting firm on behalf of their client. The following agenda of the meeting was distributed at the beginning of the meeting:

1. Introduction

2. Purpose of Meeting

3. Description of Potential Assignment

4. Basis for Evaluating Candidates

5. Ground Rules for Solicitation

6. Agency Credential Presentation/Discussion

7. Compensation Discussion

8. Questions and Open Discussion

The objectives of the meeting were laid out as follows:

- to meet agency management on an informal basis
- to provide very confidential background briefing material and an outline for the final presentation so that if you are selected to continue in the competition you can begin immediately to prepare your materials
- to ask you some questions about your agency's philosophy, operations, and experience

- to provide you with key written criteria for selecting an agency
- to outline the general ground rules in the selection process we are following and answer any questions you may have, if you are still interested in soliciting our business

The client's consultant provided a written description of the kind of PR firm the client wanted; the functions it would be expected to perform; agency staff and top management involvement required; managerial attitudes; and method of measuring and evaluating public relations performance. Objective criteria for selecting a PR firm were stated. They included:

1. Capability in both public affairs/corporate communications, product publicity, and media relations
2. Location in the client headquarters city and New York
3. Absence of conflict as defined by client
4. Agency size requirement in terms of billing and number of employees
5. Experience in terms of size and types of clients served

The consulting firm specified that this was as open competition with all agencies having an equal chance of being selected, and stated that all agencies would receive the same treatment, information, and consideration. They explained that there were two stages in the competition: the get-acquainted meeting and a half-day meeting with the client selection committee a few weeks later. Three or four finalists would be asked to make presentations after which a prompt decision would be made.

Agency Top Management

The appearance of agency top management in the initial get-acquainted meeting is critical. Since a firm is, in a very real sense, a reflection of its leadership, the participation of the agency head provides valuable insight into the character of the firm and the way it does business. It is also important for the top client contact to have respect for and be comfortable with the agency head. There will be times in the course of the account where critical public relations problems arise or when problems between the client and agency must must be resolved. On those occasions, the senior client contact should know that the agency chief is a person they can count on.

At this first agency presentation, the agency chief should project interest in any commitment to participation in the account. However, the agency chief that hogs the stage may betray a lack of confidence in his staff. Be especially aware of promises to personally manage your account. Remember, he has a business to run and is already involved with a number of agency clients. He can be expected to be available for strategy planning and review sessions and other important meetings and occasions, but it is unrealistic to expect him to become immersed in any one account, yours included, on a day-to-day basis.

There are exceptions, of course, and special circumstances to consider. Soon after I started the public relations division of Foote, Cone & Belding, I was able to promise my personal involvement to the frozen food industry. Why not? It was our first client and I could well afford to give my personal attention to an account with a then sizeable budget of $350,000. No other competing agency head could make that promise credibly. Despite the growth of our business, I continued to personally manage the account until I left the firm five years later to become a partner in what became Golin/Harris Communications. I even carried two business cards—one as President of FCB/PR, the other as Executive Director of FACT, the Frozen Food Action Communications Team. My experience is not unique. Many heads of PR firms are still involved with clients they started with two or three decades ago. Two examples: Al Golin of Golin/Harris and McDonald's Corporation, and John Graham of Fleishman-Hillard and Anheuser-Busch.

I've always believed that in selling, as in life, honesty is the best policy. I have lost business by being honest and telling the prospective client that I could not personally direct their account and run a major PR firm. In one case, the head of a much larger agency with whom I was competing won the account with a promise that he would personally work with the client CEO. I thought the client was naive to buy such a blatant overpromise but I was wrong. Much to my surprise, Bob Dilenschneider, the indefatigable chairman of Hill & Knowlton, was able to make good on his promise. He reasoned quite properly that the CEO of this Fortune 500 company was too busy to devote much time to public relations and would involve him only when vital public relations issues were on his agenda.

Who Will Work on My Business?

The client has a right to know "who will work on my business" and have exposure to these people from the outset. Proposed account team members should be involved both in the presentation and the Q & A section. You also are entitled to know what other accounts they are working on and how much time each can be realistically expected to devote to the account. Harland Warner, executive vice-president and deputy director of Manning, Selvage & Lee, Washington, D.C., believes that staffing is so critical that clients should be provided with:

- lists and qualifications of staff—full time, free-lance consultants
- staff to be assigned to your account—qualifications and longevity with the firm
- percent of their time to be devoted to your account and other accounts they will handle
- staff or personnel backup available
- staff turnover for the past two years

  and even

- names of several former employees[4]

In addition to these "on paper" qualifications, the get-acquainted meeting gives the client an opportunity to test the intelligence of the players on the proposed account team, to observe their enthusiasm for the account, and to determine if they are the kind of people they would want to work with personally and depend on professionally.

The Post-Meeting Evaluation

After each agency presentation, time should be allowed for each member of the selection committee to complete an agency evaluation form. The agency should be scored on general capabilities such as:

- quality of management
- quality of account staff
- response to questions asked
- the questions they ask
- experience in similar public relations situations
- fit with client culture
- degree of interest in the account
- enthusiasm

Before moving on to the next agency, the group should meet to discuss "first impressions" while they are fresh in mind. A designated committee member should take notes on the discussion for later reference. It should be predetermined if those firms that accumulate the most votes remain in contention or if firms will be narrowed down by negotiation. Another imponderable factor: are all votes equal or is the senior person or client contact first among equals?

Cultural Compatibility

Consultant Al Croft says that the importance of cultural compatibility cannot be overestimated. He says that "chemistry between agency and client—often hard to discern or define, and frequently reliant on "gut" feelings—can be (and often is) the deciding factor in a firm search and one of the most important elements in a productive relationship." He points out that "corporate culture wears many cloaks. It can be billed as traditional company practices or attitudes, inherited interests, instincts and ethos, personality profiles, and other factors. However defined, culture is the essence of corporate and firm flavor, drive, and direction. It has been established and matured over a lengthy period of time and is not subject to transient variations to fit individual situations. A lack of corporate compatibility between client and agency does not deserve to be judged as *good* or *bad*, but only in terms of *vive la différence*. Where cultural compatibility does not exist in one instance, it will flourish in another. Recognizing the potential or lack of potential for such compatibility at an early stage is one of the prime virtues and hoped-for outcomes of the first, exploratory prospect–firm meeting."[5]

Evaluation Criteria

Consultant Tony Louw asked 180 clients what they wanted to find out from an agency credentials presentation. Their collective answer: I want to "feel" that the agency can do something for us. His survey reveals that client buyers look for firms that best meet these criteria in the credentials presentation:

1. Did the firm prove its accountability for specific results?
2. Did they demonstrate a working knowledge of our business?
3. Did we like them?
4. Are they strategic? Did they demonstrate leadership through ideas?
5. Is senior management realistic about their involvement?
6. Did the firm show creativity both in presentation and ideas recommended?
7. Did they present ideas relevant to our business?
8. Are we the right size for each other?
9. Is the agency a team? Do they look like they work together? Do they demonstrate teamwork by referring to each other in the pitch?
10. Did they demonstrate courtesy and honesty? Did they answer directly or waffle?

Louw found that the most effective presentations were interactive. The most effective agencies involved the client from the beginning and didn't wait to ask for questions at the end of the scripted presentation. He advises agencies not to be so buttoned-down that "you don't let them see you sweat." This shows the effort you put in for them. It shows a passion for the client as well as your recommendations.[6]

Why Agencies Don't Make the Cut

Bill Weilbacher has compiled a comprehensive list of the most common reasons why advertising agencies are dropped from the list. I have restated some of these factors that are most applicable to PR firms as questions you might want to ask yourself at this point in the agency selection process:

1. Would agency management be compatible with our management?

2. Do the agency people seem to be too aggressive, too insensitive, too "New York," too young, too old, too anxious to please, too contemplative, too uniformed, or too sedentary?

3. Is the agency too tightly organized? Is it too bureaucratic?

4. Is the agency too loosely organized to fully and promptly respond to our requests?

5. Does the agency top management have a plan for or interest in maintaining contact with top client management or does it view such contact as primarily social?

6. Does the agency have a plan to perpetuate itself and its management skills?

7. Is the agency experienced in the product category represented by our account or in the type of work required by the account?

8. Does the agency have a recent history of excessive or unexplained account losses?

9. Does the agency have a recent history of extensive account gains and seem overwhelmed with servicing its new business?

10. Does the agency show signs of instability?

11. Has it retained few or none of its accounts of five or ten years ago?

12. Does the agency seem interested in getting the account?

Looking at the Broad Picture

After their get-acquainted meetings, some companies "fall in love" and may feel they are ready to foreshorten the process and pick an instant winner for their account. It's always wise to postpone the decision until you have an opportunity to separate salesmanship from a rational review of the firm's qualifications, and check them out with people who know them better than you possibly can at this early point in time.

Harland Warner concludes that "a fancy audiovisual presentation, a nice brochure and a meeting with the principals may give you a feel for the organization, but it probably will not give you sufficient information to make a good decision. You need more than a 'gut reaction.' He recommends taking the following steps to develop a broad picture of each firm under consideration:

- Interview the account executive as well as the firm's principals.
- Check that it is not a "revolving door" where staff or clients come and go frequently.
- Find out what former employees or clients have to say about the agency.
- Investigate the firm's financial situation. Does it pay its vendors and suppliers on time, or does it have a cash flow problem that could handicap its work for you?
- Ask how the firm will measure and report its success. Does it provide management reports and does the format satisfy you?[7]

Putting It Together

The purpose of the credentials meeting has been to eliminate the least suitable firms and reduce the short list to a manageable list of the best qualified finalists. Clients remember firms that stand out in the crowd. Among those that don't make the cut are the faceless firms that look and sound so much like all the others that they fail to establish a distinctive personality and presence.

Three important factors, then, will help you determine which agencies will become finalists. They are: (1) the agency's ability to meet your criteria, (2) your reaction to the agency's management and account team as future business partners, and (3) your "due diligence" to verify agency claims and answer questions raised in the presentation.

The search committee must determine if there is a need to delay a decision on the finalists in order to get answers to critical questions before polling the committee. The committee should then be reassembled to arrive at a decision on who the finalists will be.

References

1. O'Dwyer, How to Hire and Get the Most from Outside PR Counsel," 142.

2. Croft, "Anatomy of an Agency Search," 36.

3. Joe Marconi, *Getting the Best from Your Ad Agency*, (Chicago: Probus Publishing Company, 1991), 41.

4. Harland W. Warner, "How to Select a Firm: A Different Approach," *Public Relations Journal* (October 1983), 29.

5. Croft, "Anatomy of an Agency Search," 36.

6. Antoni Louw, presentation to PRSA Counselors Academy, May 1990.

7. Warner, "How to Select a Firm: A Different Approach," 29.

CHAPTER 6

The Final Assignment

The short list of finalists is usually comprised of three to five PR firms. When the short list is finalized, you will again have the pleasure of telling the chosen few that they have made the cut and the unpleasant job of informing those that have been eliminated. You will want to call and then write the losers to thank them for their efforts. You will want to call the winners to personally congratulate them and invite them to make a formal presentation.

This call should be followed immediately by a letter that covers the ground rules of the presentation: i.e., time, place, the specific problem to be addressed with appropriate background material, the designated contact person, and a list of other company executives who will be present at the presentation. The letter should note if the presentation is limited to the agency's strategic approach to the account or if the company will expect a detailed tactical plan. If so, you should indicate if you are willing to pay the agency for such a plan.

If the presentation is to focus on how the firm would specifically approach the account, each firm should be given specific information on a public relations problem. The term "problem" is appropriate and not necessarily negative. The company may not have an immediate problem such as a product recall or public challenge to its policies but its "problem" may be how to use public relations to maximize awareness of a new service or product. The company wouldn't be hiring a PR firm if it didn't have a problem.

To obtain the best agency response to the problem, the client must be willing to provide access to privileged company information including confidential research. This requires that each PR finalist firm be asked to sign a confidentiality agreement. The client should also offer to arrange for the firms to meet face to face with key resource people. In the case of a marketing public relations program, this would include product manager and market researchers.

Recently I took a class of graduate students to a major automotive company where student teams, acting as competing PR firms, replicated a real-world client briefing experience. They were shown the prototype of a car to be introduced in two years. Presentations were made by the chief designer, engineer, and product manager to the entire group. Then each group was permitted time to meet with these key individuals. Students and all faculty engaged in the project were required to sign confidentiality agreements. Theirs was a rare experience. Far too few companies will share this much privileged information with public relations firms they are considering hiring to handle their most important assignments. They should decide to share enough information to enable the agency to approach the subject intelligently, while not giving away highly sensitive information that would give aid and comfort to the competition.

Joint Briefings

In the real public relations world, these information-gathering meetings are generally held separately with each of the competing agencies. However, I have participated in joint briefings for competing agencies. This is sometimes done by governmental or quasi-governmental bodies to save time and assure that all contestants have the same information. I also have attended meetings with pharmaceutical companies where scientific research is presented and even with a toy company where a marketing executive took the agencies through the "story line" of a new action figure line.

The Problem/Solution Scenario

The client should be willing to provide agency finalists with enough information to elicit an informed and focused response. At the same time, they should recognize that only one firm will be chosen and that the eliminated firms will have been exposed to confidential company information. To avoid this problem, some companies have created hypothetical situations, the response to which will demonstrate how the PR firm thinks and how it would approach a similar real-life situation.

> **Example**: In a few months, a respected medical journal will publish the results of a research study that will demonstrate a major new health benefit of one of our food products. How would you design a program to identify our product with this research and broadly communicate the newly discovered benefit to customers, opinion leaders, and the trade?

Speculative Presentations

There is sometimes a thin line between responding to a problem and being asked to fully develop a speculative presentation. There are arguments for and against speculative presentations. Ideas are the PR firm's most valuable product. Many agencies believe that it is inappropriate to be asked to give away its ideas and be paid only for implementation which is of less intrinsic value to the client. The situation is not analogous to advertising where under the commission system, the agency begins to reap financial rewards when the commercials or ads run. In other words, there is no windfall inherent in execution of PR programs. The agency's compensation is based on the time spent carrying out the program. While most public relations firms object to making speculative presentations, many will reconsider if they are told that only those willing to make a spec pitch will remain in contention.

Compensation for the Presentation

When the assignment is self contained—for example, public relations support for a company event or the introduction of a new product—the client should be willing to pay the finalists for their speculative ideas. This is usually a flat amount to cover staff time and expenses. Typically, the agency spends most of this amount on expenses, including travel, research, presentation tools, and leave-behind materials. While the payment hardly ever pays for the tremendous number of hours invested in the pitch, the willingness of the client to compensate the agency sets a positive tone that is likely to generate better work and a better going-in working relationship with the winning firm. Another client benefit of compensating agencies for the pitch is that the client is, in effect, buying the agency's ideas, which become their property.

One way to determine compensation to is pay the agency the equivalent of one month's fee (or one twelfth of the anticipated fees for professional time). If, for example, the PR budget for a new product introduction is $120,000, including $60,000 in agency time and $60,000 in expenses, the agency would receive $5,000 to develop the speculative presentation.

The Public Relations Audit

Many PR firms refuse to do speculative work on the professional grounds that they cannot provide professional counsel without the time and access to learn more about the company. They often suggest being paid a flat fee to conduct a communications audit. The communications audit is an assessment of attitudes of the company's key stakeholders—its employees, shareholders, neighbors, customers, suppliers, local, state and federal government agencies, advocate groups, the media, financial analysts, community leaders, and others—concluding with strategic recommendations, a course of action, and a budget. This is a reasonable response when the PR firm is being engaged to conduct a multi-faceted corporate public relations program. It might, however, be more appropriate after a firm is picked as their first step in designing the public relations plan.

Chase Manhattan's Fraser Seitel cautions his corporate PR peers to resist the PR firm's request to first "get to know" the organization by interviewing top management because it consumes executive time and because he says some consultants use the "management audit" as a guise to get to higher ranking executives for future considerations. He admits that there's nothing wrong in concept with first researching the beliefs and aspirations of senior management, but warns that "you, as a spokesperson and conscience of the organization should approach the management audit with caution or at least question its necessity."[1]

Time to Prepare

The finalist agencies should be given adequate time to prepare their presentation. It has been a constant complaint from PR firms that they are brought in "at the last minute." This might be necessary when a totally unexpected company crisis occurs; for example, when a food company discovers a contaminant in its product or when a company finds it necessary to defend itself from a takeover attempt. However, most public relations work is concerned with building long-range relationships with the company's "publics," both internal and external. In these situations, the client company can afford to give competing agencies adequate time to develop a public relations strategy. Many companies hire PR firms to provide public relations support for marketing new and existing products. Their marketing plans are developed over a year or more. The company should have its PR firm in place in time to contribute to and be integrated and budgeted into the total marketing plan. That means that the search for the PR firm should begin months before the program is to be executed. PR firms should be given at least a month to develop a speculative pitch.

The Critical Period

Most clients make a point of assuring all competing agencies that they have an equal opportunity to win the account. But the client may well be predisposed toward an agency before the presentation because of the effort they have demonstrated to immerse themselves in the client's business and the public relations problem at hand. They so convince the client of their genuine interest in the business that they come into the finals not only with greater understanding of the problem and what should be done to address it, but also with high grades from the client for their initiative.

On a postmortem from a client we did not win, I was told that the winning firm personally interviewed not only everyone in the division's marketing group but its research and development people as well. They even asked for and got permission to talk to the company's distributors and dealers. I was told "I think they even interviewed the janitor." The firm also attended a trade show before the presentation to observe how the sales department presented the product line to customers. The client told me that because of this firm's extraordinary display of interest in the account and its knowledge of the marketing problem, there was "no contest" on which PR firm to pick. I had to agree.

Some agencies go home from a thorough briefing and become so engrossed in their presentation that they are never heard from again until their final presentation. Others stay in touch by phone. There is, however, a thin line between calling to ask legitimate questions that will better enable them to address the client's problems and finding excuses to call. Frequent callers who waste the client's time risk becoming pests.

Reference

1. Seitel, "How to Hire a PR Firm, "A 145.

CHAPTER 7

The Pitch

The client should decide where the final presentations will be held—at the agency, the company, or a neutral place like a hotel. Hotels are often used when client personnel and agencies are coming from different locations. Trade association presentations are typically held at association headquarters or in hotels near the airport, since executives from several companies in different locations plus the agency staff are involved. This also allows out of town agencies to fly in and out on the same day. Since it is difficult to assemble the committee members, the decision of which agency to select is often done on the spot and agency principles are asked to be available so that the winner can be advised and the relationship initiated.

The benefits of having each agency present at company headquarters is that it enables the process to be foreshortened and a full complement of decision makers, including members of the company's top management, to attend. It also puts all agencies on a level playing field with respect to facilities and equipment. Wherever the presentation is held, it is essential that all (or at least the same) committee members and voters attend all presentations. This assures the competing agencies that they are being fairly judged vis a vis the others. It also assures that there is a true consensus in the selection decision.

When the presentation is in the home office, steps should be taken to assure that home office participants' calls are screened.

There is nothing more disconcerting to the agency (or to the committee if it seeks top management approval) than to have the CEO's secretary slip her a note which takes her out of the room to accept "an urgent phone call." If the selection of a PR firm is not a priority, she should not attend. I have seen a CEO do paperwork in back of the room during the agency pitch and another use the slide show to grab a catnap in the darkened room. This is the agency's big moment for which it has worked so hard. It is disconcerting and deflating to the agency to see their hard work so received.

As with the get-together meeting, no more than two agency presentations a day should be scheduled. If the key players can only be assembled on one day, you may be required to squeeze in three presentations. Realistically, two hours should be allotted for each presentation to cover set-up time, some amenities, presentation, questions and answers, breaking down A/V, gathering up exhibits, handshakes, and time for each member of the team to score the agency. Some firms will want to hold an initial discussion after each presentation. Don't forget to make room during the day for coffee breaks, "pit stops," and sandwiches.

PR firms must be skilled at adapting to unfamiliar surroundings. Some smart agencies make arrangements to visit the presentation room prior to the presentation. Companies employ a wide variety of AV equipment and size is not necessarily a clue as to the sophistication of the A/V set-up. Some major presentations for major companies are made in less than grand surroundings. On the other hand, some smaller companies appropriate space-age board rooms or sophisticated training facilities for the pitch.

Meeting on Unfamiliar Turf: Ten War Stories

War Story #1:   In the tense final moments before a major presentation, the client contact informed me that the auditorium was equipped with the latest rear screen projection equipment. That meant that we were found furiously flipping over all 200 slides rather than shaking hands when the company executives filed into the room.

War Story #2: On another occasion, a member of the search committee tripped over the slide projector cord, overturning the projector, spilling and scattering a full tray of slides on the floor. A time-out had to be called while we struggled to reassemble the slides in order. The resultant presentation was an acid test of the improvisational skills of our presentation team. Despite some surprises in the order of the slides and a few that were backwards and upside down, the presentation must have made some sense. We got the sympathy vote and the business.

War Story #3: To this day, I don't understand how slides can melt in a projector but this actually happened to me during an important presentation. The projectionist waved frantically from the back of the room to get my attention. I must say my audience was most sympathetic as I described what was on each slide in an improvised performance reminiscent of comedian Jackie Vernon's hilarious radio narration of his summer vacation slides.

War Story #4: Do you remember the Federal Express spot where the adman's slides didn't arrive on time and he had to resort to making finger shadows on an empty screen? That commercial always reminds me of the pitch I made with an associate at a macaroni company in Jersey City. We took one of New York City's zillion yellow cabs to the train station. After paying the driver and watching him disappear in city traffic, I asked my associate if she had our overhead transparencies. "No," she said, "I thought you had them."

By the time we arrived at the company our office called to say that the cab driver had found our material and asked his next fare to call us. Trouble was that our office was in Chicago, the slides were in New York, and we were in Jersey City. We had little recourse except to "call an audible" and to "walk the client through the book." The pasta people didn't seem to miss our creative slide presentation and—happy ending—we won the account.

War Story #5: I once participated in a combined advertising–public relations presentation that was so important that it was videotaped for some top company executives who couldn't attend. When they reviewed the tape, they saw our presentation team leader trip over a cord and knock over an easel, sending dozens of charts off into the audience of unamused executives.

War Story #6: Then there was a presentation in the board room of a leading home appliance manufacturer. The chairman, president, and various other top executives welcomed us and we took our seats around the board table. Portraits of generations of the company's leaders hang in this dignified setting. Making himself comfortable, my partner leaned back on his swivel chair, executing a near-perfect pratfall. Our very gracious and very proper hosts pretended not to notice as he picked himself up off the floor and began the presentation.

War Story #7: Then there was a presentation I made for the Berlin tourism account. Not only was the presentation made in Berlin to a committee of politicians and bureaucrats who didn't understand much about public relations, but most of the committee didn't understand English either. Their restlessness was obvious. My attempts at humor fell on deaf ears. Their questions were in German and their conversation mostly directed to each other. A few days later, we learned that we were a hit with the state senator who was the biggest hitter in the room and we got the account.

War Story #8: I was once involved in a pitch for the marketing PR account of the Peanut Advisory Board. Having successfully competed for other food trade association accounts, we decided that a touch of show business would make our presentation stand out. In addition to themed leave-behinds, we rigged up a robot as a peanut character, suggesting that he appear at trade shows representing the industry. But we saved our best for last. As we completed our presentation, the doors of the room swung open, and to the tune of "You Deserve a Break Today" came a crew from the local—Tifton, Georgia—McDonald's, led by the local store manager. Each member of the committee was served a "Nutty Sundae," as we announced for the first time anywhere that our client McDonald's would serve chopped peanuts on their sundaes. We expected the news that the the world's largest restaurant chain would be buying millions of pounds of peanuts would not only win the account but arouse a standing ovation. The response was dead silence. The committee members assumed that their staff had ordered refreshments and asked us to continue. We had apparently misread the committee. The voters were not the typical marketing executives we knew from the frozen food, canned food, and pet food industries. They were no-nonsense peanut growers from Georgia, Alabama, and Florida, unused to such nutty antics. When our time was up we packed up our robot, headed north, and awaited our rejection notice. We were not disappointed. Adding insult to injury, we received a bill weeks later for the use of the slide projector and VCR the client provided for the presentation.

War Story #9: I have not had remarkable success pitching public relations programs to grower groups. I introduced a presentation to the California Strawberry Advisory Board with a brief agency history. I mentioned that we were the public relations subsidiary of an advertising agency that was 104 years old. The committee included a number of Japanese-American growers, one of whom opened the Q&A section by asking me if any of the founders of our parent firm were alive and, if so, why weren't they with us. I learned that day that the Japanese do indeed venerate elders.

War Story #10: A trade association I once pitched had assembled busy executives from a half dozen companies for one day only and was on such a tight schedule that the association executive announced that he would ring a bell when time was up. We got in under the bell on that one but we weren't so lucky with a beer company on a equally tight time schedule. Their agency requirements included service in several cities. Since we didn't have offices in one key city, we brought in the head of the out-of-town agency to pitch with us. He came on late in the presentation and despite all of our rehearsals, got so carried away that he was still selling when our alloted time expired. He didn't notice that the company's PR director had left the room to tend to a PR crises. Poor timing was a deciding factor in the decision to pick the other guy.

Key Questions to Ask

You will be evaluating the agency not only on their specific response to the problem you have asked them to address, but on a number of key factors which are predictors of success potential. Some are technical, some professional, some personal. Some clients and consultants evaluate firms not on the specific tactics they recommend at the pitch but on how they approached the assignment, their PR problem-solving process, and "how they think." They recognize that, given more information and more research time, the PR firms might refine their strategic approach and therefore their tactical recommendations. The client that makes its pick totally on the basis of tactics developed over a few weeks by a firm lacking sufficient information may be looking for a quick fix rather than an in-depth approach to their public relations problem.

While many of the questions you ask will relate to the specifics of the agency's recommendations, others should be designed to go below the surface. Some of the these questions will arise spontaneously. Some may have occurred to committee members based on their previous exposure to the firm, the specific PR assignment, and the requirements of the client-agency relationship.

The Counselors Academy of the Public Relations Society of America recommends that these questions be addressed some time during the presentation:

1. How long will it take the PR firm to get up to speed on your account?

2. What reporting/measurement methods are to be used?

3. Who is the PR backup when the key person is not available?

4. Does this key person understand your organization's needs and ask intelligent questions?

5. Does this key person appear to have the supervisory ability to lead the account team?

6. Does the key person have any experience in your organization's field?

7. How is the chemistry between you?[1]

Clients' Advice to PR Counselors

A panel of corporate public relations executives shared their views of "How and Why Public Relations Firms are Hired or Not" at the 1990 Spring Conference of the Counselors Academy of the Public Relations Society of America. Their views are not only instructive to agencies selling their services but to clients who are buying. In fact, Gary Tobin, vice-president public affairs, American Express Information Services Corp., told the counselors to "imagine you are your own client." He said that clients look for agencies that:

- market themselves better by giving speeches and writing articles and op-ed pieces
- position their expertise credibly—every agency can't do everything
- are around people with needs—at trade shows, civic groups, etc.
- put a premium on local expertise (His company prefers PR firms that know the market to those that say "we just happen to be located here.")
- make agency principals part of the presentation and then part of the account team
- don't abandon me to an inadequate account team (He said that clients should be wary of account teams based on the firm's needs rather than the client's. Clients don't like to get the feeling that they are getting "leftover people.")
- listen to or at least pretend to listen to the client instead of doing all the talking (Tobin said clients don't want the PR firm to dominate every discussion during the solicitation and after they get the business. He said "We want someone to talk to and to give us therapy.")
- know when to shut up after they've made the sale

Tobin concluded that the best way for PR firms to get new clients is to keep the old ones. He said that if you keep old clients happy, they will refer you to other corporate public relations executives.[2]

Another panelist, Jeanette McDonald, vice-president Communications, Dun & Bradstreet, offered ten rules to agencies who are selling and to clients that are buying agency services:

Rule #1: Address the client's agenda.

Rule #2: Present a strategy, not tactics.

Rule #3: Be sure you can execute what you recommend.

Rule #4: Show actual people who will work on the account.

Rule #5: Give fresh ideas for current problems. Avoid case histories that aren't pertinent to my problems.

Rule #6: Address measurement by establishing success criteria in terms of meeting objectives. Are key messages covered? Are third-party endorsements coming from targeted parties?

Rule #7: Clients look for quality, speed, and price but you can't win on price alone. Clients know they get what they pay for.

Rule #8: The references you give don't count.

Rule #9: Treat your client like an equal. Don't be afraid to argue for something you believe in, but be sure to be an excellent listener, too.

Rule #10: Make sure your client knows you need access and honesty to be effective.

Finally she cautioned that "public relations is like a marriage. A relationship gone sour can be very messy."[3]

The Importance of Style

Management consultant Chester Burger advises clients to gauge whether the personality of the PR firm is compatible with their own. "Some clients prefer a super-aggressive firm. Others like a more conservative approach. Which is right for you? Everything else being equal, the right match can make the difference between success and failure."[4] The client will inevitably evaluate the presenting agencies on style as well as substance. The matter of style is closely related to fit. Conservative clients will respond more favorably to thoughtful, reasoned analysis of their problems, especially if the assignment is essentially corporate, as opposed to marketing.

If the client decision makers are marketing executives used to advertising agency pitches which emphasize "creative," they interpret a glitzy dog and pony show presentation as indicative of the creative spark the agency would bring to their public relations program. Recently a public relations firm won a "shootout" for a major public relations account by building a stage set representing one of the client's stores. PR firms soliciting marketing PR accounts often theme their presentations and provide buttons, badges, tote bags, and other paraphernalia and decorate their leave-behind books with the theme graphics. With the right audience, these touches work. But the agency has to know its customer.

Non-Program Factors

On successful occasions, I have gained some insights into some of the non-program factors that influenced clients to eliminate finalists. One new client told me that while I had been in touch with members of the committee continuously over the Christmas holiday, the head of a competing firm appeared wearing a fresh vacation tan when the final presentations were held in early January.

At another presentation, we asked to see the presentation room the day before the finals. We weren't alone. The first agency had set up a battery of a dozen computer-programmed slide projectors. Our A/V equipment consisted of a series of informal overhead transparencies. We thought we were dead in the water and we were wrong. One of the reasons the agency with the projector armada was eliminated, we were told, was that they came off as big spenders. If they spent that kind of money on a new business presentation, the committee figured that they might spend the client's PR budget recklessly.

Agency preparation for the pitch means practice, practice, practice. The agency must not only know what to say but how long it will take to say it. The client is almost always working on a tight time schedule. If there isn't another agency in the other room ready to present, there may be other urgent company business to tend too.

A Soupy Sale

In the early 1980s, legendary advertising man David Ogilvy, whose agency Ogilvy & Mather represented a number of Campbell Soup brands, wore another hat as consultant to Campbell's then-CEO Harold Shaub. Sales for the company's flagship condensed soup line were flat and Ogilvy advised Shaub to hire a public relations firm to conduct "a massive PR program" to motivate consumers to eat more soup. A committee under the chairmanship of the U.S. company president was formed to select a PR firm. After the five finalists made their presentations in Camden, the committee made its selection and reported it to the CEO. Not so fast, Shaub urged, "Why don't you run it by David Ogilvy?" Running it by Ogilvy required then-marketing services director (and now president of Campbell North America) Herb Baum to fly to Ogilvy's villa in southern France with the five leave-behinds for his review.

"Have you come to a decision?" Ogilvy asked.

"Yes," Baum replied.

"Was it unanimous?"

"Yes," again.

"Then there is no reason for me to read these."

Good-bye and good luck. Baum boarded the next plane to Philadelphia and Golin/Harris was informed that we had the business. The choice proved to be the right one. The account endured for more than a dozen years and through three Campbell CEO's and three changes of agency ownership.

References

1. Louw, presentation to Counselors Academy.
2. Gary Tobin, presentation to PRSA counselors, May 1990.
3. Jeanette McDonald, presentation to PRSA Counselors Academy, May 1990.
4. O'Dwyer, "How to Hire and Get the Most from Outside PR Counsel," 139.

CHAPTER 8

Evaluation Criteria:
The Agency View

Advice on how to select the right PR agency is plentiful from the agencies themselves. Some public relations firms have drawn up their own criteria "to help clients" evaluate agencies. While these lists can provide helpful reminders to experienced clients and help educate those new to the agency selection process, the PR firm that provides this kind of advice can be expected to emphasize the importance of areas of its greatest strengths. A multi-office firm, for example, will advise clients to evaluate PR firms on the seamless service and control they can offer nationally. On the other hand, a PR firm that is part of a network of affiliated independent agencies will emphasize the value of local ownership and community involvement of its partner firms. A large firm can be expected to emphasize the importance of an array of services and specialties and the advantages of one-stop shopping for all PR needs. A small shop will stress its personal service and in-depth specialization.

At least one major firm distributes its own checklist before the prospective client hears final presentations. While it may be an effective selling tool in some cases, clients can expect an emphasis on the agency's strong points.

Advice from a Small PR Firm

Alan Towers Associates, a small, New York-based public relations firm, even publishes a booklet for clients called *Selecting a Public Relations Firm*. The selection criteria they recommend favor the small to mid-sized firm. Towers suggests that clients ask the following questions when choosing a firm:

1. *What do you need? Do they have it?*   Different communications objectives require different public relations skills and knowing your goals is the first step in finding a firm to help you reach them. Even the largest firms excel in one or two areas and are average in others. A common mistake is thinking a reputation earned in one discipline of a firm applies to all specialties. Ask what percentage of the agency's work is done in each category.

2. *Where do you look?*   Some excellent public relations firms keep a low profile and are barely visible. They keep low profiles behind their clients, so you'll need to do some digging. Check with companies you see communicating well, often, and distinctly.

3. *Things may not be what they seem. What really matters?*   Be careful not to over-rely on results you're shown. Bear in mind you'll be seeing only success stories. There's no assurance of repeat performance. Rather, you should see a deliberate, consistent marketing strategy that moved a program steadily toward a planned objective. Does the agency demonstrate problem-solving ability and original thinking?

4. *What about agency size and client longevity?*   The larger agencies will offer a wide range of experiences and services. They'll have depth and staffing to handle heavy workloads over wider geographic areas. But smaller shops can often work more efficiently and personally. The length of an agency's relationships offers a clue to how well it performs.

5. *What you see isn't always what you get. Who will work our account?*   If a firm's senior executives are "pitching" your account, find out how much of their time you will actually get. Ask about the rest of

the staff that will be servicing you. Meet them. Make sure the firm isn't overloaded.

6. *What are our exact costs?*   Ask for a complete rundown of the service you can expect for your fee and what will be extra. You should also be given a pretty good idea of the additional out-of-pocket expenses you can expect.

7. *How important will your business be to them?*   Generally your account will be as important as the size of its fee—not just the dollar amount, but how your fee compares to others at the shop. Did the firm discuss why the account was right for them?

8. *What are some alternatives to specific program proposals?*   It will be months before an agency really begins to understand your business. Asking for an elaborate presentation of what the firm intends to do for you forces the agency to guess before it knows. Ask instead for an outline of the major communications issues facing your organization, some potential responses to them, and the time it will take to see change.

9. *Is your account properly managed? How will you know?*   Ask if the firm provides some kind of calender or flow chart of activities to be performed in each month or quarter. Spell out in advance how much paperwork you'll require and what procedures for approving the agency's ideas will be necessary. Ask for time records with each statement.

10. *Roll up your sleeves. What is our role in the relationship?*   PR firms need frequent interaction and contact with clients. Be prepared for a partnership and make sure you are prepared to provide the agency with direction and more information that it needs.[1]

Advice from a Large PR Firm

As might be expected, the "Basic Guidelines for Choosing the Right PR Firm" recommended by Hill & Knowlton, one of the Big Three firms offering public relations services on a global scale, suggests criteria favoring a large, multi-national, full-service firm. Robert L. Dilenschneider, president, and Michelle H. Jordan, senior vice president for international business development, give these suggestions to companies choosing a PR firm:

1. Make sure that a good match exists between the outside agency and your internal staff. How exactly do your want the outside agency to amplify your communications capability? Are the roles of both inside and outside staff clearly defined in an overall communications plan? Have top managers—in both line and staff functions—bought into this plan?

2. Watch how an agency candidate behaves in the selection process. Do they respect your need for confidentiality? Do they anticipate your needs for planning and budgeting? How thorough are they in explaining how the agency works and introducing you to the people who will actually work on the account?

3. Use your firm's own strategic goals as the chief measure to evaluate agencies you are considering. Not infrequently, we will steer a potential client to a firm which is smaller or much more specialized than a Hill & Knowlton. Sure, we want all the business we can get which will satisfy the client and which will be rewarding for us. But, sometimes that fit just does not exist. We have been repaid for our candor by firms later choosing us as counsel when the scale of their needs increased or their strategic direction changed.

4. Measure the competitive awareness of a candidate agency. Access to information is a much bigger part of public relations today. Without penetrating and focused "competitive intelligence," it is hard to position your firm in the marketplace with unique memorable messages. Does an agency have strong routine systems to gather data? Can it describe to you how it used intelligence to help advance the interests of other clients? How will it make use of intelligence to build programming for you?

5. Study a candidate agency's client list rigorously. Does the agency have a real feel for your business and industry sector? This is not just a "learning curve" question—often it signals if good chemistry is likely to exist between the agency and your firm. Construction business experts and consumer marketers are different breeds, as are high-tech innovators compared with people in the entertainment industry.

6. Assess the agency's ability to grow with you. One of our clients in the United Kingdom knew that it was going to be a player in Europe and the Middle East in a matter of just one or two years. Strategically, its identity would also change because of pending acquisitions and it needed a firm which could help reposition the business with the new identity. We were chosen, quite frankly, less for our ability to serve the company's then present needs, but because we could make a decisive contribution to the future of the firm.[2]

Werle's Evaluation Form

Perhaps the most comprehensive evaluation form to help corporations and associations select the right public relations firm was developed by Chuck Werle, president of Werle & Associates, Chicago. Werle brings the perspective of more than 25 years on both the corporate and agency sides of public relations with Hill & Knowlton, Leo Burnett, First Chicago, and Miller Brewing Company.

The form asks clients to score prospective agencies on 65 attributes on a 1 to 5 point scale in these rating categories: client service, creativity, account team credentials, industry knowledge, program management, affiliations, and counseling experience. Werle tailored his system to be used by product managers and other corporate executives who have never hired a public relations firm as well as those who have past experience working with agencies.

The Werle & Associates "Public Relations Agency Evaluation Form" follows.[3]

References

1. *Selecting a Public Relations Firm*, booklet published by Alan Towers Associates, Inc., 1987.

2. Robert L. Dilenschneider and Michelle H. Jordan, "Basic Guidelines for Choosing the Right PR Firm," *Public Relations Quarterly* (Spring 1991), 13.

3. *Public Relations Agency Evaluation Form*, Werle & Associates, Inc., 1991.

WERLE ⬧ ASSOCIATES, INC.

PUBLIC RELATIONS AGENCY EVALUATION FORM

Use the following criteria to rate each contending agency. Give 1-5 points (5 is highest) according to how greatly you value each attribute. Add points to determine individual category score. Grand total (maximum 325 points) will be sum of all category totals.

Agency:_____ Contact:_____

PRESENTATION SKILLS

____ Active role by account team
____ Did their homework
____ Showed creativity
____ Utilized A/Vs effectively
____ Used relevant examples
____ Degree of management involvement
____ Followed our guidelines/agenda/time
      constraints
____ Enthusiasm/confidence
____ Comprehensiveness

____ **TOTAL (MAXIMUM 40)**

CLIENT INTERACTION

____ Responds to client calls
____ Prepares for meetings
____ Meets deadlines
____ Keeps client informed

____ **TOTAL (MAXIMUM 20)**

CLIENT SERVICE CAPABILITIES

____ Interpersonal skills
____ Client reporting system
____ Service evaluation process
____ Familiarity/experience with our
      business
____ Competency
____ Management commitment
____ Account team experience
____ Risk of potential client conflicts
____ Our importance to agency

____ **TOTAL (MAXIMUM 45)**

CREATIVITY

____ Awards during past five years
____ National honors
____ Idea development
____ Esthetics of client samples
____ In recognizing opportunities
____ In facing communications challenges

____ **TOTAL (MAXIMUM 30)**

ACCOUNT TEAM

____ Level of experience
____ Years of client service
____ Years with agency
____ Enthusiastic/confident
____ Ability to represent us
____ Team leadership

____ **TOTAL (MAXIMUM 30)**

PROGRAM IMPLEMENTATION

____ Agency track record
____ Flexible
____ Schedule development
____ Scope of program

____ **TOTAL (MAXIMUM 20)**

WERLE ✲ ASSOCIATES, INC.

MEDIA CONTACTS/PLACEMENT SKILLS

____ Rating by press contacted
____ Proven national media coverage
____ Proven local media coverage
____ Reputation with trade media
____ Access to columnists, editors
____ Writing/editing skills
____ Quality of "pitch" letters

____ **TOTAL (MAXIMUM 35)**

FINANCIAL MANAGEMENT/BUDGET

____ Fee structure
____ Budget review process
____ Hourly rate range
____ Billing system
____ Accounting procedures

____ **TOTAL (MAXIMUM 25)**

AGENCY AFFILIATIONS

____ Access to marketing support
____ Member of established network
____ Scope of network affiliation
____ Reputation of network
____ Ad agency connection
____ Independent

____ **TOTAL (MAXIMUM 30)**

PROGRAM ANALYSIS

____ Measurable results
____ Ability to apply findings
____ Frequency of evaluation
____ Relevance to client objectives

____ **TOTAL (MAXIMUM 20)**

REPUTATION/REFERENCES

____ Evaluation by current clients
____ Comments from previous clients
____ Accreditation by/affiliation with
       professional organizations
____ Rating by peers
____ Image in community
____ Credibility with vendors

____ **TOTAL (MAXIMUM 30)**

GRAND TOTAL: _____
                 (MAXIMUM 325)

Comments:_____

_____

_____

NOTE: This evaluation form was developed by the professional staff of WERLE & ASSOCIATES, INC. and may not be used without prior written permission of agency management. For further information, please contact Chuck Werle, President/CEO, at 312/649-4858 or write to W&A, 150 E. Huron St., Chicago IL, 60611 (after June 1: NBC Tower, 455 N. Cityfront Plaza Dr., Chicago IL, 60611). ● 1991.

CHAPTER 9

And Now a Word from Our Client

What factors do clients believe are most important? In 1990 Geduldig Communications Management, Inc., conducted a survey of the heads of PR at Fortune 500 companies. They attempted to discover not only what corporate people say but what they do. That is, how they actually spend their dollars with PR firms. Alfred Geduldig first asked the corporate group "How do you choose which agencies to interview before making a final selection?" The response was:

references	41%
personal experience	31%
publicity	9%
other	13%

Of those who cited references, more than half identified "other corporate professionals" as their principal source. Peers within their own industry were also an important base of references, as were others within their own company. Only one of 39 respondents asked an advertising agency for a reference. One asked a lawyer.

Geduldig notes two other interesting points. First, that nearly ten percent of the respondents said that articles, written by or about PR firms, were a factor in screening agencies. Half of that 10 percent were among the largest companies that responded. And second, that the "other" category included references to mailings, conventions, directories, and the like. If the bottom two categories are combined, agency promotion of one sort or another accounts for about 20 percent of the response.

What Is and Isn't Important to Clients

Next, respondents were asked to gauge their methods for selecting the winners. Twenty-seven criteria were ranked on a five point scale from vital to unimportant. In the survey, four elements emerge as vital in agency selection. They are:

1. people
2. presentation
3. writing
4. conflicts

"People" came as the overwhelming response. The quality of the firm's staff—their creativity, their professionalism, their pragmatism—was the key factor cited by corporate PR leaders. "Chemistry" and "enthusiasm" are top-ranking factors in the presentation, and the quality of writing continues to rank high on the list. Finally, virtually all of the respondents said they would not do business with a firm that had a direct conflict with their company.

Cited as "very important" but not vital to clients were:

1. counseling skills
2. media contacts
3. willingness to accept project work

On the other hand, factors rated as "not very important" were:

1. full service capability
2. the presence of a local office where the client is located
3. size of other clients
4. national coverage
5. organization
6. markup of expenses

Many firms like to say they offer full service and nationwide offices, but corporate PR chiefs responding to this survey say these qualities aren't important to them.

Rated by the respondents as "unimportant" were:

1. low bid
2. hourly rates
3. independent ownership
4. network membership
5. prestige of clients
6. training capabilities

Surprisingly, at the bottom of the list was price. Corporate PR directors reported that "low bid" was the least important criterion used in selecting an agency. These conclusions reflect what the respondents *say* was compared to what they actually *do*.

PR Spending Levels

Geduldig asked the corporate PR directors for details of their PR spending levels, their patterns of spending, and the ways in which they used PR firms. Not surprisingly, the figures show a high correlation between the size of the company and its PR budget, staff size, and agency fees. In terms of total spending alone, larger companies appear to be the best prospects for both larger PR firms and well qualified smaller firms. Because these corporations report using an average of more than three agencies and spending over 70 percent of their agency budget on projects, smaller firms are not necessarily locked out because of an incumbent "agency of record" or a retainer arrangement.

Finally, the survey found that clients used agencies in the following categories:

Financial/IR	26%
Product/Marketing	24%
Corporate Image	23%

Community Relations	10%
Internal/Employee	10%
Other	7%

Geduldig notes that corporate PR directors are not the only buyers of PR services in many corporations and that in many corporations, the marketing department may buy far more PR than the PR department itself. He cautions that the figures may greatly underestimate marketing PR's share of the pie.[1]

Counselors' Academy Survey

Criteria used by clients when engaging outside PR counsel were further documented by a 1991 survey of members of the Corporate Section of the Public Relations Society of America. The survey was conducted for the Counselors' Academy of PRSA by Savitz Research Center, a Dallas based marketing research firm. The survey measured the degree of importance corporate public relations placed on factors in selecting an outside counsel. The net result of this exercise produced three factors that weight most heavily in a choice: (1) the key account people assigned to the work; (2) the firm's experience in the client industry, and (3) the ability of the firm to meet deadlines. Two other factors that enter into the mix are the firm's experience in a particular subject and the client's perception of how the outside firm's key people and client personnel will "fit" in a collaborative effort.

Seventy-two percent of the respondents of this survey reported that their firms use outside PR counsel. About one-fifth of the sample reported retention of outside counsel on an annual contractual basis, with a similar number reporting usage on an "as needed" basis depending on work load or on special assignment due to an unusual or unforeseen need.

On average, those using outside firms in 1990 engaged an average of 2.4 firms of which 29 percent were engaged for the first time. By far, the most dominant reason (cited by 54%) for adding a new firm was to obtain the services of a specialist that was not available among the client's other counselors. An additional one-third of those who added a new firm last year said they did so to increase their outside resources. Interestingly, only one in seven said a new firm was engaged to replace an incumbent (as is most frequently the case with new advertising agency appointments). Almost half of the new engagements were awarded without competitive bidding.

Among the entire sample of respondents, over half (55%) say they will accept new business solicitations from counselors on a selective basis while 37 percent do not accept such solicitations.

While the advice these clients offer to PR firms soliciting their business is diverse and instructive, the words "do your homework" and "know our business" recur repeatedly among the responses.

Top line results of that section of the Savitz survey dealing with attitudes towards and usage of outside counselors (public relations firms) are reproduced as Addendum A of this book.[2] Verbatim responses to the survey are included in Appendix B.

Other Decision Makers: Other Criteria

It should be remembered that the respondents of both the Geduldig and Counselors' Academy surveys were top PR officers. They may believe that they are capable of handling most PR programs in-house. Therefore, it cannot be assumed that they will agree with a decision made elsewhere in the company to hire outside PR counsel for a critical corporate PR role or for a highly visible PR program. Their responses may indicate that they see counseling firms as a threat to their department.

While the PR director may be a member or even chairman of the selection committee, he may not be the key decision maker in a particular PR search. In the search for a principal corporate PR counsel, the decisive votes will be cast by the chief executive officer. His perception of the ability of an agency to counsel with him on vital issues impacting the corporation and his personal comfort level with agency top management may be of paramount importance to him.

Similarly, marketing PR programs may be evaluated by marketing executives whose selection criteria may differ markedly from that of their corporate PR people. They can be expected to be especially interested in how well the PR program will fit into an integrated marketing plan and their vote can be expected to be influenced by the agency's marketing knowledge and skill.

Quaker Public Relations Agency Review Questions

In order to help its product managers evaluate PR firms, the consumer communications department of Quaker Oats Company provides them with a list of questions that "represent the important areas you'll want to think about to determine who will be the best public relations partner for you on your business."

Capabilities:

Is the agency big enough yet not too big?
If they talk about offices in other cities, do they demonstrate how they have worked with them in the past?
Is their revenue growing more through new clients or more business with current clients?
What other [packaged goods/food] clients do they have?
Do they keep their clients long term?
Do they do more project work or annual programming?
Are the case histories applicable/relevant to you?
Do they have a sense for what is newsworthy?

Strategic thinking:

Do they work against objectives or set up their own?
Do the tactics follow the strategy?
Are they focused?
Do they understand your business?
Did they follow directions from the briefing?

Creativity:

Are the concepts compelling?
Do the creative ideas follow the strategy?
Are the concepts clever?

Do their creative ideas work for the product/company image?

Do they execute with good taste and ensure quality?

Management style and effectiveness:

Do they do their homework or is there a lot of puffery?

Are they formal/informal, organized, concise, and service oriented?

Do they demonstrate strength in handling details and follow through?

Do they demonstrate flexibility?

Were they well rehearsed? Did they run the meeting?

Account team:

Are you comfortable with the team?

Are they excited about your business?

Do the team members handle themselves professionally?

Are they top heavy (too senior) or bottom heavy (too junior)?

Do they have a sense of humor?

Results-orientation/measurement:

How do they evaluate the success of a project?

Do they set measurable objectives?

What is their attitude about results? Are they used to addressing the issue?

Are they asking the right questions to help you understand what public relations can do for you?

Do they exhibit knowledge of the research discipline?

Value of the presentation:

Did they attempt to reach our target audiences?

Were there creative, useful ideas worth pursuing?

Did we learn anything we didn't already know?

Would they be effective in reaching the media?

Did they accomplish the assignment?

The marketing team members are provided with the following Public Relations Review form:[3]

PUBLIC RELATIONS AGENCY REVIEW

Agency _____ Date _____

Agency Capabilities:

Size and scope: _____

_____

Revenue trend: _____

_____

Extent of resources/expertise: _____

_____

Clients: _____

_____

Case histories: _____

_____

_____

Presentation: _____

_____

Strategic thinking: _____

_____

Creativity: _____

_____

Management style and effectiveness: _____

_____

_____

Account team: _____

_____

_____

Results-orientation/measurement: _____

_____

_____

Value of presentation: _____

_____

_____

References

1. "What Corporate Public Relations People Seek in Selecting Public Relations Agencies," study conducted by Geduldig Communications Management, Inc., April 1990.

2. "PRSA Corporate Section Members Look at Public Relations Now and Down the Road," a survey for the Counselors Academy conducted by Savitz Research Center, Inc., April 1991.

3. Quaker Oats Company, 1991.

CHAPTER 10

Picking the Winner

Good vibrations, intuition, comfort, and gut feel are important in picking the winner but the decision is too important to rest on such subjective factors alone. I believe it's absolutely essential for the client to carefully craft a list of criteria which are most important to the company, prioritize them, and incorporate them in an agency evaluation form.

The evaluation form enables each member of the review committee to register individual impressions of each agency finalist. While the cumulative point score may indicate a clear winner, it should not be the sole criteria for agency selection. The total score may mask a considerable division of opinion about a firm. The high score may be the result of very high ratings by one member of the committee while other members give the firm only average ratings. Then too, there is the matter of whether or not all votes are created equal. In companies dominated by a strong leader, that person's vote may, and in all likelihood should, prevail. If the boss isn't satisfied with the selection, the new agency may get off on the wrong foot. Progress will by stymied while the boss consciously or unconsciously sets up roadblocks to success. In a situation like this, everybody is the loser.

In other companies, responsibility for the public relations program may be pushed down to lower management levels. Here it is essential that the designated client contact person be sold on and be comfortable with the agency selected. The contact person's vote may be more important than those of the other voters and may be based on a reasoned case for the selection of a firm that didn't win on points.

Since no two companies and no two public relations assignments are alike, it follows that there can be no standard formula for evaluating public relations firms. What is important is that the criteria reflect as accurately as possible the client's expectations. Some MBA-driven companies will put the greatest emphasis on strategic thinking, while others are more interested in tactics, i.e., "The Big Idea." Still others will heavily weight media or street contacts. In virtually every situation, compatibility or "fit" is deemed critically important.

In any case, it is recommended that very careful consideration be given to the criteria upon which agencies will be evaluated. Taking time to arrive at a consensus on the importance of criteria being evaluated and weighting those criteria to the client's priorities is a critical step that sometimes does not get the attention it deserves. Yet it is the best way to aid the rational selection process and avoid "seat of the pants" judgments.

Developing a Rating System

In their book, *What Happens in Public Relations,* Gerald Voros and Paul Alvarez recommend that clients develop their own list of key selection criteria and rate each agency on how well it has performed in each area as demonstrated in the presentation, in conversations, and in written material. They suggest that the following system can also be used to evaluate the agency during the time it is serving the company. It includes a rating system and a checklist of factors to be considered in making up your own list of important criteria.[1]

Importance Rating	Points	Performance Rating	Points
Critically important	5	Superior	9–10
Extremely important	4	Above average	7–8
Very important	3	Average	5–6
Somewhat important	2	Below Average	3–4
Of minor importance	1	Inferior	1–2
Not applicable; of no importance	0		

CHECKLIST OF FACTORS

I. Internal Performance

    A. Working knowledge of

- The public relations business

- Public relations planning

- Public relations research

- Public relations evaluation

- Marketing and public relations

- Legal aspects of public relations

- Sales promotion

- Production-print and broadcast

- Industry, economics, and social trends as they fit client structure

    B. Specific performance

- Overall planning and implementation judgment

- Quality of client contacts and reporting

- Frequency of client contacts and reporting

- Preparation of client billing and income forecasts

- Writing skills

- Presentation skills

- Ability to organize and direct meetings

- New business development
- New business presentation skills
- Overall creative ability in the following areas:
  News and feature writing — print and broadcast
  Speech writing
  Booklets and other printed materials
  Audiovisual presentations
- Programming
  Media placement—print and broadcast
- Ability to have productive relationships in client areas with:
  National media
  Local media
- Degree of understanding in the following areas:
  Financial communications
  Employee relations
  Community relations
  Product publicity
  Government relations
  Press relations
  Consumer relations

II. Client Performance

    A. Depth of knowledge of:

- Client products service
- Client marketing process
- Client competition

    B. Ability to secure client approval on work and budgets

    C. Acceptance at top client levels

    D. Acceptance at middle client levels

    E. Ability to keep client informed of public relations work

    F. Ability to demonstrate public relations success to client

    G. Acceptance among client's public relations group

Use of the Rating System

A variation of this rating system was used by a major packaged goods company to evaluate three finalist PR firms competing to
conduct a major marketing public relations program for one of
the firm's divisions. The firm weighed each factor on a scale from 1
(low importance) to 10 (very important). Then each firm was rated
on each factor from 1 (poor) to 5 (excellent). In other words, an
agency receiving the highest rating 5 on a factor weighted 10 would
receive 5 × 10 or a total of 50 points on that factor. An agency
receiving the lowest rating 1 would receive 10 points. This form
evaluated competing agencies on 11 criteria as follows:

- Strategic thinking (10)
- Quality of program recommendation (10)
- Ability to produce results/execute plans (10)
- Ability to work/plan against strategies and objectives (10)
- Resources/contacts/research capabilities/staffing (9)
- Creativity with focus (8)
- Initiative/sense of urgency (8)
- Regional marketing experience (7)
- Firm/staff experience—have handled large national consumer products companies (7)
- Ability to integrate communication with ad agency (6)
- People talent/skills/style (5)

Like all PR programs, special considerations were considered
when drawing up the list of criteria. For example, a PR firm was
being selected for a division of the company whose sales are skewed
regionally so regional marketing experience was of importance.
Since it is a major advertiser, the integration of the PR program and
advertising campaign was also considered important.

While the selection committee achieved a consensus on this
particular search, it is interesting to note that virtually all members
of the selection committee noted on their evaluation forms that

"people talent/skills/style" should have been weighted 10 or greater. The importance of people is as critical in selecting a public relations firm as in selecting an advertising agency, perhaps even more important since the key agency contact person is likely to be as much implementer as manager. While the typical advertising account director's function is to coordinate the work of creative, media, and research functions and interface with the client, the typical account director in a public relations firm is likely to be responsible for copy and media placement as well as client contact.

Similarities to Ad Agency Criteria

While the work of advertising agencies and PR firms are dissimilar, the personal and professional qualities clients seek in their advertising agency and PR firm are virtually identical. Foote, Cone & Belding has compiled a composite list of criteria used by advertisers to select agencies. With the exception of media buying (and the difference in media planning in advertising and PR), much of the list applies to public relations, specifically marketing public relations. The list in order of the importance of selection factors follows:

1. Creative work that is effective is selling the product
2. Really understands problems associated with client's business
3. Careful with client's money
4. Creative flair
5. Responsiveness of the account group
6. Media planning
7. Media buying
8. Accessibility and involvement of top management
9. Helpfulness in developing strategic marketing plans
10. Use of research in planning
11. Providing a full range of services
12. New product expertise

13. Strong regional or international branch offices
14. Global or multinational advertising capabilities

ANA Evaluation Guidelines

In its guide "Selecting An Advertising Agency," the Association of National Advertisers suggests that ad agencies be evaluated on a scale of 1 (low) to 6 (high) in three principle areas: (A) Strategic Communications Planning; (B) Tactics/Service Capabilities; and (C) Compatibility/Confidence Impressions. With the exception of the few specific references to media planning and creative planning, the ANA's suggested agency selection evaluation criteria reproduced here could apply equally to the evaluation of PR firms, particularly those being evaluated for marketing public relations assignments.[2]

AGENCY SELECTION EVALUATION CRITERIA

A. Strategic Communications Planning
1. Demonstrated an in-depth *understanding of their clients' markets*, the marketing problem/opportunity, the marketing objective, and significant influencing trends/conditions, including competitive factors
2. Demonstrated an understanding of *competitive factors* in the market discussed
3. Demonstrated an understanding of the *customer/purchaser/user*
   a. client company (case histories)
   b. our company
4. Articulated measurable communications objectives (*accountability*)
5. Demonstrated an understanding of the role of different *communications tactics* in meeting marketing and communications objectives
   a. case histories
   b. problems given
6. Recognized and endorsed the need for an appropriate use of *research/results evaluation*
   a. case histories
   b. problems given

7. Demonstrated a *strategic planning approach* to the marketing/communications case histories discussed
   a. problem/goal definition
   b. planned, systematic approach (overall)
8. Demonstrated in their approach to the *given problem* a sense of its *relativity to other areas of our business* (our brands, new products, etc.)

B. Tactics/Service Capabilities
   1. Demonstrated an innovative/effective *creative communications execution* program consistent with objectives and strategies
   2. Demonstrated an understanding and acceptance of the varying *pace* and *demands* of handling their accounts
   3. Demonstrated *initiative*
   4. *Anticipated* needs and problems
   5. Understood the need for *cost efficiency*
   6. Prepared to put forward a *point of view* and defend it, using adequate suppports
   7. Demonstrated in their *approach to our problem* an understanding of the nature of the marketplace(s) in which we compete
      a. purchasers/users
      b. competitors
      c. retailers
   8. Demonstrated an understanding of our particular *competitive advantages/disadvantages* and a way of working with these particulars
      a. to help us move toward realization of both brand and corporate goals
      b. to separate us in a meaningful way from competition, i.e., positioning
   9. Overall/other comments or notes

C. Compatibility/Confidence Impressions:
   1. Related well to us
      a. executive management
      b. marketing management
      c. advertising management
   2. Appeared to work well as a team, coordinated through one client contact point
      a. account management
      b. other
   3. Articulated their ideas well
      a. agency management

b. account management
c. other
4. Were good listeners
5. Maintained high standards of performance
6. Demonstrated a realistic capability and generated a feeling of confidence in their ability to manage our account over an extended period of time
   a. services available
   b. personnel available
   c. attitude right
7. I'd like to work with this group.
   a. agency management
   b. account management
   c. overall
8. They feel like "winners."

Importance of the Leave-Behind

It is important to block out sufficient time after each agency presentation for each member of the selection committee to fill out an evaluation form or otherwise record impressions. Sometimes the chairperson will convene a meeting of the selection committee immediately after the final presentation to select a winner. Others will delay the committee's deliberations at least until the next day to give the members time to review the agency leave-behinds.

The leave-behind can make a critical difference, especially if it's a close call. Some public relations firms tend to overproduce their leave-behinds. In my book *The Marketer's Guide to Public Relations*, I point out the necessity of producing clear, concise leave-behinds.

Not long ago, public relations proposals were ponderous selling documents that covered every idea of everybody connected with its writing. They were regarded as exercises in persuasive writing—the more excess verbage the better. It was widely assumed that the decision makers would read every word of the proposal, no matter how long and detailed and give gold stars on how well it was written. It was felt that the readers would be impressed by the heft of the document and by the sheer energy that went into its making. The bulk of the document was a recitation of ideas to gain media coverage with little attention paid to how well these ideas supported marketing objectives and strategies. The "laundry list of ideas" approach generated by public relations firms was based on the assumption that among them there should be something the client would buy.

Most of today's marketing public relations plans are more precisely tuned to marketing strategies and presented in the language of marketing.

Public relations jargon and detailed descriptions of public relations mechanics are disappearing. The purple prose has been reduced, if not eliminated. There has been a realization that the client wants only the "facts" and will not wade through a tome to find them. The leave-behind is nearly identical with the oral presentation, but contains additional information and detail necessary to support the recommendation. Since most oral presentations are of 60 to 90 minutes duration, including questions and answers, time constraints require that the plan be focused, concise, and easy to understand. Most "go" or "no go" decisions are made on the effectiveness of the oral presentation and the ability of the presenters to defend the recommendations.[3]

While these observations were applied specifically to marketing public relations proposals, they apply equally to corporate public relations proposals.

Committee members use the leave-behinds as a quick way to refresh their memories and compare points made by the competing agencies. The leave-behind then should be a user-friendly quick reference. Public relations firms routinely tell clients at the outset of their presentation that there is no necessity for taking detailed notes since everything they will cover is in the leave-behind. While on some informal presentations the agency may elect to "walk the client through the book," they usually distribute the leave-behind at the conclusion of their formal presentations and before the question and answer session. They believe this helps keep the client's attention focused on their ideas and prevents them from tuning out and skipping to the budget recommendations.

Some enterprising PR firms have been known to send their written proposals to the client before the presentation. However, most firms run true to form and are editing, rewriting, and rearranging their presentations up to the last minute. I recall putting the finishing touches on a particularly important presentation late one night. We retired to a neighborhood restaurant for a midnight snack where we ran into, of all people, the sales team of one of the other finalist PR firms. I recall the momentary sense of panic I felt when they told us they had submitted their program to the client earlier that day. To this day, I'm not sure if they were putting us on. If not, the early submission gambit didn't help. We got the business.

Evaluating Written Proposals

Time constraints of the selection committee members or the need to get started on the program may necessitate making a decision immediately after the finalist presentations are made. In other situations, the committee may want a few days to study the leave-behind. The Chester Burger Company has developed the following standards for evaluating written proposals. They suggest that each of the following points be scored **yes, no,** or **does not apply**:

1. Organization of proposal

    a) Does it follow suggested outline?

    b) Or does it suggest why not?

    c) Does it address all issues?

    d) Should it be rejected as incomplete?

2. Planning (including creativity and applicability)

    a) Is background research (if any) relevant?

    b) Are objectives clear and to the point?

    c) Are target audiences defined correctly?

    d) Do strategies relate to objectives?

    e) Are concepts creative, attention-getting?

    f) Does proposal seem cost-effective?

    g) Does it suggest measuring specific results?

    h) Does the proposal measure the right results?

    i) Should the client reject for lack of understanding?

    j) Reject for poor planning?

3. Clarity of presentation

    a) Is proposal clear, concise?

    b) Are illustrations appropriate, effective?

    c) Is proposal tailored to client needs?

    d) Are case studies germaine?

    e) Is proposal free of errors?

    f) Should client reject for errors?

    g) Reject for poor presentation?

4. People and outside firms (e.g., market research)

    a) Are PR firm's people fully qualified?

    b) Are outside firms (if any) worthy of client?

    c) Have outside firms agreed to this proposal?

    d) Should client reject for quality of people?

    e) Reject for quality of outside firms?

5. Comments and Observations

Based on the comments, the Chester Burger Company then asks committee members to grade the proposal on a scale of **A**, **B**, or **C**.[4]

And the Winner Is . . .

Now the moment of truth has arrived. It's time to pick a winner. The members of the selection committee should have gained a knowledge of and a feeling for each of the contesting firms. They should be prepared to evaluate each on the basis of its experience, strategic thinking, specific skills, the way it does business, the quality of its people, its corporate compatibility, and its response to the public relations problem your company has asked them to address.

The committee chairperson opens the meeting by outlining the selection procedure. It is essential to complete the committee's work with a free and open discussion. While PR firms who have advanced to the finals will put forth their best efforts, their best simply might not be good enough to make the final cut. The exercise of picking a winner then often begins with a process of elimination.

After this first elimination and with the choice now narrowed, the chairman may call for a vote to get a sense of the committee's direction. The evaluation form is a valuable tool, but upon discussion it may be learned that the firm that leads on points may lack depth of support and enthusiasm. While there are times when there is a clear winner, in most instances the vote is not unanimous. Picking a winner frequently is an exercise in the art of negotiation. It's time for those who strongly favor one firm or the other to present the best case for their choice. Their arguments may win the support of those holdouts who are still unsure or undecided. The future role of the advocates in the program and their experience with public relations firms may carry additional weight.

While the committee is charged with making a decision, there are some rare cases where it is unable to choose from among two firms with strong support. On those occasions, a delegation may be selected to personally call on the heads of the two finalists to address key concerns and answer key questions which will differentiate the finalists. The subcommittee of key players may be empowered to make the decision or to report back to a reconvened session of the committee as a whole where the final choice will at last be confirmed. On even rarer occasions, the decision may be made to employ more than one firm to handle specific parts of the program. I participated in one competition where a pharmaceutical client decided to employ one firm to reach the medical community and another to reach patients. On another occasion, a broad corporate public relations program was split between separate agencies to handle internal and external communications.

Delivering the News

The agency has been selected. The time has arrived to deliver the good news and the bad news. The client contact person has the pleasure of informing the winner that it has the business. He also has the unenviable job of telling the losers that another firm has been picked. During the solicitation process, personal relationships develop, compounding the difficulty of letting down the losers.

The losers should be advised of the decision by a personal phone call to the agency head, followed by a formal letter of appreciation. The decision is anxiously awaited. Unless they know they blew the assignment, most agencies are optimistic by nature and like political candidates, expect to win. They have invested their blood, sweat, and toil in the pitch and now it's time for tears. The losers may express disappointment but most will recognize that no decision on something as ephemeral as agency selection is forever. Hope springs eternal that the winner won't work out or that there will be need for a second agency. Such agencies will take up the client's often expressed offer "stay in touch" in order to remain top of mind for next time.

Post-Mortems

However, some firms may not see it that way. Frustration may give way to indignation. The rejected suitors may lose their cool. The surest way to certain oblivion is to express incredulity at the client's decision. Questioning the client's judgment is the last way to remain in future contention. Yet some agency chiefs have done just that. Better judgment would lead to wishes of good luck to the client and sometimes even the winning agency.

The client should expect that the losing agencies will ask where they came up short. They may not be satisfied with the customary "it was a close decision and we felt that any of the finalists would do a great job for us." They may ask for a *post-mortem* on the basis that they want to know what they could do to fix agency shortcomings or improve their presentations the next time out. While the client is necessarily anxious to get back to work and get started with the new agency, many decide to take time to visit with the losers in return for the effort they put into their unsuccessful quest for the account.

The agency may believe it wants to see itself as these others saw them. But the post mortem can be a sobering experience. I've never liked to make predictions on the outcome of an agency competition but there was this one where I thought we were so good as to be unbeatable. When I was told that the business was going to another agency, I was crestfallen and asked for a post-mortem. The key client contact person agreed not only to discuss our presentation but to share the written evaluations of the selection committee. The ratings were generally within a shade of the winning firm. However, one voter wrote (and it still hurts): "Their presentation was simplistic, long, and philosophical. Also I was underwhelmed by their people including top management." My firm fared far better in the search described in the next chapter by Dennis Spring, the consultant who conducted it.

References

1. Voros and Alvarez, *What Happens in Public Relations*, 216.

2. *Selecting an Advertising Agency: Factors to Consider, Steps to Take*, published by Association of National Advertisers, 1979.

3. Thomas L. Harris, *The Marketer's Guide to Public Relations*, (New York: John Wiley & Son, 1991), 65.

4. Bill Cantor, Experts in Action: *Inside Public Relations*. (New York: Longman, 1989), 402–403.

The Anatomy of a Public Relations Search and Review

Dennis Spring
President,
Spring Executive Search, Inc.,
and Spring Associates

Sony Corporation of America, a major company and force in the consumer electronics industry, changed dramatically in the frenetic decade of the eighties. It was evident that Sony's marketing technology and product message needed a fresh, new perspective for the nineties. Its U.S. electronics business had grown three-fold in the previous five years to nearly $5 billion. The Consumer Products Group alone was introducing more than 400 new products a year. The marketing and corporate communications departments had undergone many internal changes and had metamorphosed into something that was difficult to get your arms around. The corporate communications department had too few people handling more work than ever before. The marketing groups were diversifying, entering new markets, and creating new markets at a rapid pace. The window between the introduction of new technologies was closing. Competition for market domination was intensifying.

A senior corporate communications executive pointed out to me how an effective public relations program relies heavily on integrated marketing techniques. In the seventies, when Sony began to actively promote its products in America through external public relations, these techniques were virtually unused. Eventually the discussion turned into a request for my firm, Spring Associates, to conduct a communications audit and subsequently a public relations search and review. It took us more than two months to conduct personal interviews with over a dozen key players in the corporate communication and marketing departments. The interview process included everyone from the president of the Consumer Products Group to the public relations coordinator.

Just as important were the editorial opinions from several important consumer electronics and business editors at pivotal trade and national publications. To round out the audit, selected individuals representing competitive organizations and vendors were also questioned. The public relations agency search and review for the Consumer Products Group grew out of the recommendations in the communications audit.

For the first time since retaining public relations counsel 18 years before, the group was prepared to formally evaluate its public relations programs and agency. The mere thought was painful to some Sony personnel. The actual act would be even more painful. Relationships had formed, alliances had developed, friendships evolved—everyone realized that the review process could mean either the enhancement of an existing agency relationship or the beginning of a completely new one.

As in any dynamic organization, opinions differed. A few Sony executives felt that the incumbent agency had done an excellent job in the past and would continue to do so in the future. The review team's response remained flexible. No pressure was exerted to force any divisional executive into participating in the review. They were free to continue using the services of the incumbent agency for their division.

A meeting with senior members of the corporate communications department was held to map out a search and review strategy. The initial criteria in the agency review called for agencies that had experience in consumer electronics and/or the hi-tech business. Questions about agency size, office locations, depth of experience, agency culture, staffing, and budgets surfaced as primary considerations. Agencies with an office in New York, home of the national media, ranked high on the priority list. The ability to station an agency account executive at Sony headquarters in Park Ridge, New Jersey, on a part-time rotational basis was on the list of criteria.

A presence, or a willingness to have a presence in California and Chicago was also a consideration.

Finally, the company wanted an agency that would view the Sony account as important to their firm. The probability that the fee income would increase dramatically over the years was highly likely given Sony's record of rapid growth.

In addition to the search strategy, we drew up a comprehensive list of review evaluation criteria. The list kept the review team focused and directed throughout the process. In the early stages of the search, the review team was composed of the director of corporate communications and the vice-president of advertising and communications of the Consumer Products Group. The incumbent PR agency was given equal opportunity to compete for the Sony business throughout the agency search and review.

The agency search and review was strategically designed to approach the review process in small, timed steps. Each phase was designed to complement the phase preceding it, by whittling the list of agencies down until the finalists emerged. Originally, Sony preferred to remain anonymous. So we began the review process by sending a one-page letter to more than 30 agencies which fit our minimum qualifications for inclusion. The purpose of the letter was to announce the search, explain why the recipient agency was under consideration, ask for information needed immediately, and request a standard capabilities packet about the agency. (See sample letter, Exhibit A).

A full-blown multi-media presentation was deemed unnecessary in the initial phases. There were too many agencies to consider in the first round, and we didn't want to become distracted with slick presentations before we had a sense of the agency behind the presentation. All the information we received was carefully scrutinized by the review team. We rated the capabilities and history of each firm and its suitability as a potential PR agency for Sony.

The group of agencies was whittled down further. A questionnaire went out with a request for written responses. The questionnaire explored areas of strategic and creative development, quality control evaluation, billing procedures, and more. We were

SPRING
EXECUTIVE
SEARCH, INC.
212-685-3080
ONE MADISON AVENUE
NEW YORK, N.Y. 10010

December 26, 1989

Name
Title
Company
Address
City, State Zip Code

Dear

We've been retained by a company who wishes to remain anonymous at this time, to assist them in conducting a Public Relations Agency Search and Review.

Using relative size, reported fee income, satellite office locations and overall client mix as our preliminary screening criteria, your agency and several others have been chosen for consideration.

Our client could best be described as a: multi-billion dollar, international, New York metro area based, consumer electronics and high technology products marketing company.

Our client will be looking for a comprehensive public relations program which will include: special events, press conferences, press releases and kits, feature stories, trade and consumer media placement, case histories and generally, a pro-active, creative, strategy and marketing communications program designed to maximize public relations opportunities.

The first year projected net fee budget will be approximately $600 thousand with at least as much in out-of-pocket expenditures. These budget figures are approximate and offered as a guide only.

We would like to know if you have a Los Angeles presence and if your agency is currently working with a consumer electronics or high technology firm.

If you're interested and want to be included in this Search, please send us informational and capabilities materials about your agency by January 11, 1990.

You will be notified if more information is needed. After our client has reviewed your materials, five to ten agencies will be selected as Semi-Finalists. The target date for final presentations and the naming of an agency of record is March 1, 1990. Good luck.

Sincerely,

Dennis Spring
President
ds:lb

trying to get a sense of management style. Would the agency's management approach be compatible with Sony's? Sony Corporation of America can be described as a fluid, vertically integrated, decentralized, matrix organization that seeks consensus from its managers on all matters of importance to the company. From the beginning, it was our intention to gain a consensus among the corporate communications and marketing managers on the issue of corporate culture and chemistry fit.

Each agency was asked if it would resign any existing accounts that were actually or potentially in conflict with Sony's products. Some would. Some would not. We recognized that certain agencies have a corporate policy prohibiting the resignation of one account for another. In some cases, we felt compelled to cut those that had conflicts and would not state that they would resign the conflicting account if they won the Sony business. It was a sticky area, but the consumer electronics business, much like the computer business, is highly competitive. All information about products in the research and development as well as the marketing stage must be carefully guarded.

As search consultant throughout the process, I drafted the questionnaires and other correspondence that moved between the agencies and my client. All communications, written or otherwise, filtered through me. I sought help from the appropriate person at Sony on any inquiry that I couldn't confidently answer. Since fairness is the hallmark of an agency search, it is critical that the consultant act as the information funnel through whom all information and communications flow. This ensures that all parties are consistently given the same information, so that no one agency can gain an unfair advantage over another at any stage in the search process.

Careful evaluation of the capabilities material followed, with a review of responses to our first questionnaire and discussions about the agencies' cultures and organizational management styles. The list of agencies under consideration eventually shrank from more than 30 to 14. The remaining agencies were informed that the anonymous client in our agency search and review was Sony Corporation of America and were asked to honor Sony's continuing wish for the process to remain confidential. Appointment dates were set for specific agency personnel to meet with representatives from Sony. Simultaneously, each agency was given an agenda that included "suggested discussion topics" for the upcoming meeting. The initial meetings were held in Sony's New York office. The emphasis was on chemistry as much as content, giving the search team the opportunity to whittle the list down even further.

We scheduled a second round of meetings with the remaining agencies in their offices—a good opportunity for the search team to view each agency on its own turf. I answered or found out the answers to any questions the agency participants had regarding their upcoming meeting. Care was taken not to reveal any information that would have given an advantage over another before going into their meeting. According to members of the review team, the unusual and logistically difficult step of making on-site visits bolstered some agencies and hurt others. Was the office environment busy without being frenetic? Was the physical layout of their offices appealing? Was it an environment that was seen as conducive to creative thought? Did it reflect an "excellence" of corporate culture? Were there enough computers, word processors, and such, to speed the flow of work? These were only some of the questions that the Sony representatives tried to answer by personally visiting the agencies.

Each agency was given an hour in which to ask questions of the Sony people. The kinds of questions asked and the chemistry between client and agency all factored into the decisions that cut seven more agencies and left us with seven semi-finalists. A final questionnaire, which covered specific topics like operating procedures and policies, the creative development process and evaluation techniques, helped to bring the list of finalists down to five, including the incumbent.

Since the incumbent was familiar with Sony, we invited the other four finalists to Sony headquarters in Park Ridge, New Jersey, for a 90-minute discussion and tour. These meetings were followed with more on-site visits to each agency office by ten to twelve marketing heads of Sony's consumer products companies. Consensus by all in this process was essential. The public relations agency would most likely be working directly with each of the respective marketing heads at some point. Their input was critical.

In the final stages of the review, these finalists and the incumbent were briefed in preparation for three public relations challenges they'd be asked to respond to with program proposals. In addition to a strategic recommendation, we requested information about budgets, staffing, and timing for three case studies. The finalists were given about two weeks to prepare. During this period, two Sony representatives and I met once again in the finalists' offices to preview their proposals, offer direction, and answer any last minute questions.

The final presentations were held in a large hotel room near Sony's headquarters in Park Ridge with some fourteen corporate communications and marketing heads in attendance. There were no restrictions placed on agencies' presentation method. Slides, videos, and overhead projectors were permitted and used. Presenters were given 75 minutes for program proposals and approximately 45 minutes for introductions and questions from the audience.

The case studies were quite difficult considering the agencies' prior limited knowleged of Sony's business strategies and the time given to prepare. The questions from the marketing heads were tough but fair. As in most presentations of this type, the more thoroughly the agency researched the challenges and developed the strategic proposals, the easier it was to defend them before a questioning audience. In addition to the creative and strategic qualities of the ideas presented, the agencies were measured by their efforts to go beyond satisfying our stated requirements. Enthusiasm and presentation style of individual personnel, and of their team as a whole, weighed heavily in the voting. After each presentation, evaluation sheets were completed by the Sony personnel and an open discussion followed. Assets and perceived deficiencies were debated. All fourteen heads of marketing and corporate communications expressed their opinions—sometimes vigorously.

The debate became lively at times. The intensity of the discussions not only achieved a consensus about the relative strengths of the new contending agencies, but also clarified the weaknesses of the incumbent agency. It became clear as the debates and votes continued that change was inevitable. My role in these meetings was to keep the deliberations on course and express my opinion when asked. The final decision would rest with the Sony executives.

In the end, Golin/Harris Communications, a mid-sized agency, owned by Shandwick PLC, prevailed. Golin/Harris was selected because the consensus was that they best fulfilled the criteria of size, office locations, breadth of services offered, quality client roster, talented people, creative programs and management teams, and many other internal attributes that Sony felt were crucial to Sony's future growth as a company.

As in all agency searches of this type, chemistry and corporate culture ranked high in the entire decision-making process, yet they were the most difficult to quantify. After all the discussions about professional capabilities, technical resources, and the like, the discussion always ended with the questions: Do we feel comfortable with this group? Do they seem willing to partner and grow with Sony? This comfort factor was often given as much weight as major portions of the presentations.

A comprehensive plan was drawn up to phase-out the incumbent and phase-in Golin/Harris. For their efforts, each finalist was given a Sony Mavica camera as a gift of appreciation for the investment they had made by their participation.

Spring Associates' active involvement was officially over, although we continued to monitor the progress of the situation. The entire process, including the audit, took more than eight months to complete. To date, the results have been very positive and the relationship has already expanded to other Sony divisions. Everyone involved is looking forward to a mutually profitable, long-term relationship.

PART II

Working With a Public Relations Firm

The qualities that make a client–agency relationship succeed are basic and applicable to relationships of all types — trust, candor, knowledge of the partner, clear communications goals and objectives, and realistic budget approaches. If these building blocks are established, the results of the relationship should be mutually beneficial.[1]

CHAPTER 12

Getting Started

For the victors, the beginning of the new relationship is cause for celebration, breathless memos, agency gatherings, and toasts. Often the client may want to personally welcome the new firm by entertaining the principals and account team. The honeymoon has begun.

The agency will want the world to know of its success in landing the account. It may ask the client to issue a press release announcing the news and offer to draft it. While PR news may not be followed as avidly as advertising news on newspaper business pages or marketing columns, many PR appointments are considered newsworthy because of the size of the account, the nature of the assignment, or local interest in the client company. The news may also be of interest to the public relations trade press, the marketing/advertising trade press, and the business publications covering the client's industry.

Starting Up

The first work session will likely include revealing confidential client information that could not be shared with all of the competing agencies: for example, sensitive marketing research, new product information, and company plans that will impact the client's various publics. Based on this information, the agency may be asked to review its initial recommendations. The agency may also be given its first project assignment or assignments.

However, the initial meeting will be largely devoted to mechanics and the setting of ground rules for the new relationship. Reporting relationships must be defined. The key client and agency contacts should be identified. In many relationships, client/agency counterparts on various levels are designated while it is understood that there must be some flexibility in who talks to whom about what. Since the planning of public relations programs requires extensive fact and opinion gathering, the agency will need access to persons throughout the client organization from top management to company researchers, experts, specialists, and field people. Procedures and parameters have to be established to provide this access.

Meeting Schedules

Some agency programs require day to day contact. Others that follow on an agreed-upon timetable require less frequent contact. The tempo of the client-agency relationship develops over time. Initially the client will probably want to closely monitor the agency's activities. As the client becomes more comfortable with the agency and its grasp of the assignment, it may lessen these close tabs and give the agency greater freedom and flexibility in which to operate. However, initially it is recommended that regular review meetings be held with the client. These may be weekly, bi-weekly or monthly depending on the nature and urgency of the assignment. Overnight mail delivery and modern technology—specifically the universality of fax communication and agency computers that talk to client computers—have speeded up the communications process and have reduced travel time and cost. While this facilitates copy approvals, it does not eliminate the need for up-close and personal meetings between agency and client to share information and insights and discuss strategy, forward planning, and tactical programming. Frequent live meetings cement relationships, further team-building, and engender trust.

The public relations account service relationship can be compared to the relationship between an advertising agency and its clients. Adman Joe Marconi recommends that clients:

1. Meet with your agency at least weekly to review and fine-tune your program and be aware of developing opportunities or activities of competitors.

2. Alternate the site of the meetings. It is very healthy for the relationship to visit each other's offices frequently.

3. Make certain someone—agency or client—writes a meeting report, if only a brief summary. People remember things differently, and that can be very costly to all concerned.

4. If the chemistry is wrong, ask for changes in the account team. Not everyone is compatible, and agencies would rather change account execs than lose an account or suffer an unhappy client (which is sometimes worse than losing an account).

5. Be clear about what things cost. It is unsettling for agencies to have their invoices questioned because you don't understand what you are paying for.

6. Exchange information. Agencies should pass along columns or articles from trade publications or research reports; clients should share competitive analysis or internal communications that may in any way affect the program.

7. Define roles and protect each other. When a client has a new personnel addition or change, that individual will want to plug into the process before having an understanding of the responsibilities and reporting relationships. A common question when a new player comes on board is "how will this affect our program?" Eliminate the anxiety by making clear who does what.

8. Be ethical. That may seem obvious, but sometimes compromises are made without realizing it. Think and be careful.[2]

Top Management Involvement

In addition to frequent meetings of the client and account management teams, top management involvement should be encouraged. Chances are that agency top management promised some level of involvement in the account. They probably meant it, but unless some formal involvement is built into the program, the involvement of agency management will depend on the initiative of an agency chief with a lot of bases to cover. Chances also are that client top management has less time for casual contact with the PR firm's principal—that is unless the corporation has an immediate crisis.

Under normal conditions, the agency top managers should participate in meetings to review agency progress, present agency recommendations or discuss emerging issues or problems. Some agency heads have become personal confidants of the CEOs of their corporate clients. They are called on for advice in situations too sensitive for discussion with the account team and corporate PR staff. It's lonely at the top and the CEO needs access to an inner circle of advisors with no political or personal axe to grind. The head of the PR firm often fills that role. It's not uncommon for a professional relationship to develop into a social friendship.

Reporting Systems

A formal agency reporting system should also be set up at this point. While most clients have neither the desire to be buried in paper nor to divert the agency from the job at hand by requiring them to submit too many reports, certain reports are necessary to keep all parties informed and in sync. Many important decisions are made in meetings and on the phone. It is important that these decisions be recorded and reported to avoid later misunderstandings and dependence on recall of just what was decided. The time to catch differences in interpretation is immediately after the meeting when the report is issued and before implementation has begun and budget expended.

Some clients require monthly status reports, listing status, next steps, and due dates for each agency assignment. Other clients ask for weekly status reports, particularly where many projects are being executed simultaneously and on short deadlines. In addition to status reports which summarize activity, clients should expect a more detailed report at the completion of each major project, such as a media event, tour sponsorship, annual meeting, or security analyst appearance. These project reports provide detailed information on how the project was executed and how results were measured and an analysis on how well the objectives of the project were met.

Finalizing Financial Arrangements

In addition to setting up lines of communication and reporting systems, perhaps the most basic issue to be resolved at the initial meeting is the financial arrangement under which the agency will serve the client. First there is the matter of overall budget. The client may have predetermined and pre-budgeted its public relations program. In this case, the PR firms will have to work backwards to determine what can realistically be accomplished within this budget in terms of fees and necessary out-of-pocket expenses. This approach is applicable to programs that can be pre-programmed such as marketing public relations programs.

Typically, a broad-based corporate public relations program is more open-ended and requires greater budget flexibility. The new firm may suggest that it conduct a public relations audit before recommending specific strategies and tactics. Some clients may have simultaneous needs for immediate action in certain areas and a long-term public relations strategic plan. This might involve separate project budgets. If the time for each can be accurately estimated, an agreed-upon flat fee can be imposed. If, however, the work is open-ended, it will probably be necessary to tie agency compensation to actual hours spent on the project.

Methods of Agency Compensation

The straight fee system brings certain benefits to both client and agency. The agency knows exactly how much staff time can be applied against the account and can allocate staff personnel accordingly. This not only puts a cap on PR expenditures but assures the client of dedicated staff, immersed in their account rather than sharing staffers who might have other important priorities for other important clients of the agency. The straight fee system has another benefit to the client. He will be better able to track public relations expenses and know what's been spent, what's committed, and what's left in the budget. The fee system hassles which frequently arise over billing of unexpected time charges can undermine client/agency relationships. With the straight fee system the risk of unpleasant surprises at billing time is minimized. On the other hand, the "monkey" is on the agency's back to deliver what it promised for the fee. They may well discover that they underestimated the time involvement but are bound contractually to the arrangement they made before they really understood the time requirements of the assignment.

Even the most experienced PR firms make these mistakes. Despite experience, no two programs are exactly alike. A press conference isn't a press conference isn't a press conferenece. They can range from a no-frills news announcement to a satellite spectacular. Then, too, no two clients are alike. Some clients have great confidence in the agency to do the job with a minimum of supervision. Others are immersed in every detail. The need for more meetings, more drafts, more faxes, more phone calls, and more levels of client approvals may far exceed the norm and throw the budget out of whack. If the agency is held to the budget, this can result in making the account unprofitable and lessen agency enthusiasm. The client should recognize that the agency account manager's performance is measured not only on the quality of the work and the satisfaction of the client but the profitability of the account. No client wants to hear his agency crying and carping about money especially when it was the agency that recommended the budget and agency compensation arrangement in the first place.

Fees vs. Time-based Compensation

When I entered the PR field, the flat fee was almost universally used as the way to compensate public relations firms. In those days, clients hired a public relations firm. Period. Only the largest companies had their own internal PR departments. For the others, the agency became the total public relations resource. Times were less complicated and public relations was equated by most clients primarily with publicity. This kind of pro-active publicity today falls under the category of media relations, which is in itself just one of the relations that make up the greatly expanded public relations function. In the public relations-equals-publicity era, a flat fee was charged by the agency to obtain favorable media coverage, mostly in newspapers, magazines, and business press. The job was never easy, but the parameters of the assignment were clear. What the client wanted and paid for was "ink." We did it all for them thirty years ago for a monthly retainer of one thousand dollars, more or less. The term *retainer*, still used by some PR firms, was then and is now a misnomer. A law firm charges its clients a retainer to be on call and available when needed. Then the meter starts running. Under the old definition, a PR firm did the work for the retainer. No one thought about meters.

Today, straight fees have largely been replaced by arrangements based on actual time expended. They remain in use mostly for short-term projects which have a beginning and an end which allow the firm to accurately estimate staff time and out-of-pocket expenses in advance.

Fees are also used for programs in which each of the elements is set well in advance. A marketing public relations program may include a press party, media tour, video news release, brochure, a radio contest, press kit, and editorial visits. A budget can be established to execute this kind of program based on the agency's (and sometimes the client's) experience. The budget usually consists of two parts: an estimate of professional staff time costs and out-of-pocket expenses. Such a budget should always include a contingency to cover enhancements and take advantage of emerging opportunities. Under such an arrangement, there must be explicit agreement of what the budget covers and does not cover. The client should recognize that add-ons may increase staff time and out-of-pocket costs, requiring approval of a budget supplement.

A PR executive at a $1 billion company responding to a Jack O'Dwyer survey recommended that first-time clients might want to begin the relationship with a PR firm on a short-term retainer basis, but that this arrangement should be modified as the agency gets to understand the company and "the relationship is divided into an ongoing series of projects, each with its own goal and budget."

> What I'm suggesting is a way to split the difference between a retainer relationship which risks losing its sense of purpose, and a project relationship where the agency parachutes into a situation without having a good understanding of the context and is therefore much less effective.[3]

Harold W. Suckenik, an attorney specializing in public relations law, advises PR firms to seek a minimum monthly retainer against which hours will be applied. Additional charges are levied for hours above the minimum and unused hours kept in a "time bank" for use during busier periods. He recommends that a clause in the contract should note that the unused hours are not refundable in case the contract is cancelled.

He also advises firms to advise their clients that signing them on means that no competitive accounts will be taken by the PR firm and suggests that it be noted when competitors are turned down or resigned from in order to serve the client. The object of these statements, advises Suckenik, is to impress on the client that the PR firm is entitled to a "kill fee" if the client decides suddenly to terminate the account. The reasoning is that a lot of unbillable time will be spent learning the client's business and an early cancellation will be costly to the PR firm.[4]

Billing Rates

In negotiating financial arrangements based on direct compensation for staff time, the client should ascertain the specific billing rates for each level of agency staff. While an agency may consider the billing rates of particular individuals privileged information, it should be willing to share billing rates by job category—for example,

account director, account supervisor, account executive, media relations specialist, production manager, research director, etc. The
client should determine if the agency charges for administrative and
support services and if so, how much. Some PR firms charge for
clerical time, others cover it in their mark-up. There is at least one
firm that charges not only for its secretaries but for such amenities as
a chef and chauffeur.

PR agency staff time is based on a multiple of salaries. The
multiple varies from agency to agency but generally it is in the
area of two-and-a-half to three-and-a-half times salaries. Most agencies aim for their multiple by accelerating their multiple for lower
salaried staff and charging a lower than average multiple for senior
staff. For example, to make a multiple of three times salaries, a firm
may charge four times an account executive's hourly salary and two
times a senior vice-president's hourly salary. The agency multiple
covers overhead and profit. Overhead can also vary from agency to
agency based on location and the non-billable services it provides.

You may find an occasional PR firm that charges a flat hourly
rate for its professional staff time, regardless of who does the work,
but in these days of tighter cost controls, it's very rare and not necessarily an advantage to the client who wants the best people on his
business.

Most agencies set a profit goal of twenty percent per client and
rarely achieve it across the board. In public relations, as in all service
businesses, some accounts are more profitable than others. Today
public relations firms are becoming more bottom line oriented than
ever before. Particularly those that are owned by public companies
are under greater pressure to control costs, utilize staff more efficiently, accelerate receivables, and increase profits. An overall agency
profit margin of 25 percent is considered desirable and doable.

Agency Markup

Another source of agency income that should be discussed in
advance are agency markups. Many PR firms charge a markup for
out-of-pocket expenses. The markup is usually 17.65 percent, a
figure borrowed from gross commissions charged by advertising

agencies. The rationale for charging a markup is that the agency pays supplier bills for the client. There may by a lapse of 30 to 60 days or more before these charges are billed to and paid by the client. During this time, the PR firm, a relatively small business, is in effect financing its much larger client.

If the agency charges a markup, the specific categories for which this charge is added should be specified in the letter of agreement. In most cases, the markup applies to such items as audio/visual production, art, photography, printing, agency supervised research, and premiums, but not to agency travel expenses. Some PR firms allow their clients to bypass markups on big ticket purchasing by paying suppliers directly. Some arrange to pre-bill the client for these major expense items precluding the necessity for a markup. Some agencies do not charge a markup and in fact merchandise this as a sales point to prospective clients, but the client should be aware that they may instead charge for services such as agency support staff time which others cover as overhead under the multiple.

Some client organizations refuse to pay agency markups on the basis that the agency should be paid only for its time. They are right if the rationale for the markups is that supervision of photography, printing, and video product is excessively time consuming. Under a time-based agency compensation system, the agency is already being paid for this time. Under a straight fee system, the agency should be able to estimate the time needed for these jobs and incorporate it in the fee. However, most clients agree that the agency is entitled to a markup if they are being asked to play banker and pay supplier bills for the client.

The Agreement

Harold Suckenik points out that the document setting forth the financial arrangements under which the PR firm serves the client should be called a *contract* or an *agreement* rather than a *letter of agreement*. While the term *letter of agreement* is used frequently by PR firms, legally speaking a letter of agreement is an agreement to agree. It's the opposite of a legally binding contract. In most cases, the agreement is drafted by the PR firm. In others, the client initiates the agreement incorporating standard provisions used by the company in contracts with other service organizations. The final signed document is almost always a collaboration of input from both organizations.[5]

Accountability

In addition to detailing financial arrangements, agreements include a detailed description of objectives and strategies, action steps, timetable, meeting and reporting requirements, and methods of evaluating program effectiveness. Dr. Walter K. Lindemann, senior vice-president and director, Ketchum Public Relations, notes that "increasingly, the client spells out precise goals and objectives for a program or a campaign, and the client and agency together delineate all the criteria for measuring outputs and outcomes of the campaign. Clients are starting to build provisions into agency contracts that go far beyond just assessing how much ink or exposure clients' messages have received in the media. More and more they are also building in such measures of success as assessing knowledge, attitude, or behavior changes resulting from public relations programs."[6]

In their article "Making a Marriage Last: What Qualities Strengthen Client-Firm Bonds" in *Public Relations Journal*, Eugene P. Ritchie and Shelley J. Spector caution that "public relations is not an exact science but rather a "best efforts" business. The more the client understands those elements of the business beyond the firm's control, such as editorial decision making at news organizations, the less disappointed the client will be even when the best plans can't be achieved."

In the same article, Jill Gabe, senior vice-president, Lippincott & Marguiles, comments that it's incumbent upon the agency not just to let the client know what can be achieved, but what can't be achieved. She adds "I need to see the value for the money, what kind of effort is being put forth in my behalf, and tangible evidence of this effort."[7]

Other Provisions of the Agreement

Other provisions of the agreement might include:

- names of agency personnel who will work on the account and how many hours each will spend
- a confidentiality agreement whereby the agency requires those that work on the account to agree to treat information provided by the client as strictly confidential
- a provision that specifies that original art, photography, printed materials, videotapes, premiums, etc., are property of and should be returned to the client
- a hold-harmless clause that relieves the firm of responsibility for dissemination of false or misleading information obtained from and approved for release by the client
- a termination provision which specifies that the agreement can be terminated by either party without cause by written notice within a specified period. The period generally ranges from 30 to 90 days with 60 days the most commonly designated period. The period allows the agency to complete specified jobs, finalize billing, and reassign members of the account team.

Some firms also build in a provision requiring the client to agree not to hire employees of the agency. This precludes a client from taking the agency's public relations assignment in-house by hiring away key agency employees. This can happen when the client believes that its program is being handled exclusively by the key account person they see on a day-to-day basis and that they can save money by hiring that person rather than paying overhead for an agency.

There are occasions when the client may ask the agency's permission to offer a position to a staff member with the explicit understanding that this will not effect the agency's assignment or compensation. The agency may, in fact, be more than willing to do this in order to cement the client relationship. A dozen years ago, Campbell Soup Company asked permission of one of its advertising firms, Needham, Harper & Steers (now DDB Needham), to offer a job as marketing services director to a young agency account executive. The agency agreed and today that man, Herb Baum, is president of Campbell North America.

Agency-Department Relationships

In most, but not all client/agency relationships, the client interface is the corporate public relations department. Whether bringing in an agency was a departmental initiative or done at the request of top management, it is critical that this relationship get off on the right foot. The internal PR chief may fear, with some justification, a potential competition rather than a partnership with the PR firm. He may feel insecure in his position and see the hiring of a PR firm as a reflection of management's lack of confidence in the department. Management may indeed seek outside counsel because it believes the internal department lacks experience in handling certain situations such as crisis management and takeover defense. Management may have a more general agenda but be impressed by the firm's name, reputation, and client list and unwittingly set up a threat to the department.

The wise PR firm recognizes the sensitivity and the importance of working with rather than around the PR department. When the firm and department are allies, the department will publicly and gratefully acknowledge the agency's good work and take justifiable credit for recommending that the firm be hired and successfully managing its work. Many years ago, a new client candidly told me "your job is to make me look good." She was right, of course, and it's a lesson I have never forgotten. It's easy for an agency to bask in its accomplishments and merchandise its successes without acknowledging the client's always important contributions.

I've noticed that more than a few times, agencies have lost their clients soon after their most celebrated programs win awards and wide recognition within the PR industry. In many of these cases, I suspect it's because the agency took too much credit for the program's success without acknowledging that it was an agency-client team effort.

Ritchie and Spector point out that the first few months of the relationship is a test of compatibility. "For the public relations firm, it's a time to learn the culture and management style of the client company; to understand the business, its marketing challenges, and its management. For the client, it's a time to see whether or not the right firm was chosen."[8]

They say that during this period with all of the research, media list making, and internal interviews that must be done, the PR firm is bound to spend more hours on the account than they normally would. Most firms believe that this extra time should be viewed by the client as an investment in their successful conduct of the program. Others may agree to absorb these hours and not bill them back to the client.

"Both the client and firm need to understand this process and be flexible if either side begins to feel cheated or unsatisfied," they conclude.

Getting Off to the Right Start

Veteran public relations counselor David Finn notes that it's not uncommon for an agency to promise new clients that it will "hit the ground running" as the new public relations program gets under way. However, he points out that "PR is not something that can be turned on like a spigot or scheduled like advertising."

> It's an exploratory process in which one must establish goals, seek and sometimes create opportunities, evaluate opinions, anticipate obstacles and ways of overcoming them, and assign the most qualified professionals to initiate the activity which is most likely to achieve the best results.

He offers the following guidelines for clients to follow during the critical start-up period of a new public relations/media relations program.

Introductory sessions with the media should be low-key.   In the early stages of a new PR program, plan meetings with media representatives without any specific stories in mind to provide a foundation for future productive relationships. In a marketing PR program for a product that is not new, a long lead time is often necessary to develop new ways to achieve visibility and to fill up a pipeline with story ideas that have editorial appeal. It make take as long as six months or a year of editorial contact before results begin to appear. This requires a lot of patience on the part of the client, as well as judgment as to whether the PR people are making progress or just spinning their wheels.

Proper follow-up can capitalize on early opportunities.   Sometimes a PR program can start off with a bang: a major press conference about an exciting new product or the publication of a feature article on the company. But there must also be a continuing effort lest there be a lapse in the PR impact when the results of the initial announcement subside. PR requires constant activity, new ideas, and initiatives to sustain interest in a product or program. As time goes on, the agency and client can develop the right way to maintain this flow, maximizing results during periods of high activity and assuring continued visibility during slower periods when long-range projects can come to fruition.

Give a high priority to merchandising early results.   Everybody involved in a new PR program can feel a sense of relief, if not triumph, when the first results begin to appear. The program is working—an article has been published, a broadcast interview has taken place, a major speech has been given. The trouble is that once these become past history, one may wonder if anybody important noticed. Any form of media coverage is transitory, by definition. But the article or program need not be forgotten. An alert management will make sure that results are merchandised by sending reprints to customers, showing TV newsclips at sales meetings, featuring them at trade show displays, and by reporting publicity results in company publications.[9]

Media Relations: The Bottom Line

Clients interviewing PR firms are likely to talk about loftier targets such as changing perceptions of the company, and many PR firms present themselves as a strategic resource capable of counseling at the highest level. Yet a recent survey of PR directors at 200 major U.S. corporations conducted by Ketchum Public Relations indicates that what clients want most from their PR firms is publicity. In fact, four out of every five PR directors surveyed ranked media relations as a very important factor when choosing a public relations agency. Ketchum president David Drobis says:

> The fact is most clients still come to agencies because they want to be on the *Today* show. Other programs may spring from that, but press coverage is still the bottom line.[10]

Veteran public relations executive William Greener, former senior vice-president of public affairs at G.D. Searle, says:

> One thing you have to do well is media relations. As far as I'm concerned, if you don't do media relations well you are not a PR firm. You can be a management consulting firm and not do media relations well but you can't be a PR agency.[11]

References

1. "What Clients Seek in Public Relations Firms," *Public Relations Journal* (October 1990), 20.

2. Marconi, *Getting the Best from Your Ad Agency*, 199.

3. O'Dwyer's Services Report, 10.

4. Harold W. Suckenik, "What PR Firms Should Seek in Contracts with Clients," *O'Dwyer's PR Services Report* (February 1991), 29.

5. Ibid.

6. "The Key to a Perfect Relationship," *Relate* (undated).

7. Eugene P. Ritchie and Shelley J. Spector, "Making a Marriage Last: What Qualities Strengthen Client–Firm Bonds," *Public Relations Journal*, (October 1990), 16.

8. Ibid.

9. David Finn, "Getting Off to the Right Start in Start-up Programs," *Marketing News* (April 16, 1991).

10. "The Key to a Perfect Relationship."

11. Ibid.

CHAPTER 13

Evaluating Agency Performance

The client–public relations firm relationship is often compared to a marriage. Like most marriages, it requires constant nurturing by both partners. Eugene P. Ritchie and Shelley J. Spector point out that:

> As interpersonal relations, the bond between client and firm can be strengthened or undermined when one party falls short of the other's expectations. Open communication, mutual respect and integrity all play a part in the courtship between prospective clients and firms.

It is important to maintain these qualities for the duration of the relationship. One way to assure this will happen is to institute a formal agency evaluation program. The fact is that PR firms are informally evaluated every day by their client, but many clients have found that a structured ongoing evaluation program is the surest way to keep both the relationship and specific performance expectations on track.

Herbert Zeltner, my one-time colleague at Needham, Harper & Steers, has headed his own highly respected marketing and communications firm in New York for many years. He is the author of the 1991 update of the monograph *Evaluating Agency Performance* published by the Association of National Advertisers, Inc. (A.N.A.) In his introduction to the current edition, Zeltner states:

> In a very real sense, evaluating agency performance—or, more accurately, evaluating the health of the client/agency relationship—is an

ongoing, continuing activity. Satisfaction or dissatisfaction happens with every meeting, large and small, between client and agency; with every call report written and reviewed and confirmed; with creative recommendations presented, accepted, modified or "trashed"; with each production invoice verified, questioned and paid; with each deadline met or missed.

He points out that formal evaluations of ad agency performance began to be used sporadically in the 1950s and 1960s, increased in the 1970s, and are the rule rather than the exception today.

Similarly, the use of formalized agency and client evaluation systems has become widespread in public relations. This is particularly true in evaluating marketing support public relations programs where marketing managers are the direct client of both advertising agencies and public relations firms.

As Ritchie and Spector put it, "regular evaluation of the program and people involved is the ounce of prevention needed to keep uncertainly and excessive tension out of the relationship."[1]

Benefits of Formal Evaluation

The 1979 edition of the A.N.A. publication identified the following potential benefits of formal evaluations which are equally applicable to evaluating PR firms:

1. Both parties benefit from having a relevant agenda when they meet in review sessions.

2. The client develops a clearer understanding of agency operations. This is good preparation for making a realistic comparison between the agency's capabilities and the client's service requirements.

3. Since some aspects of the relationship are more important than others, the evaluation provides the opportunity to establish priorities.

4. Problem areas in the relationship can be set right before they become unmanageable.

5. By identifying the agency's strengths and weaknesses, there is opportunity to capitalize on the former and shore up the latter.

6. Each evaluation produces performance benchmarks which provide the basis for subsequent reviews.

7. The evaluation process encourages self-examination by the agency. It also provides and opportunity for the agency to speak frankly about any client actions or attitudes which are impeding progress or jeopardizing the relationship.

8. Wasteful activity, loose cost control, and other inefficiencies that might be traced to the client or the agency can be identified and corrected.

9. The evaluation gives top management of both the client and the agency the chance to judge their junior executives and assess their current effectiveness and their potential for growth.[2]

Criteria for Evaluation

Paul Mulcahy, president of CSC Advertising, Inc., Campbell Soup Company's in-house advertising company, has for many years been the client contact for both his company's advertising agencies and PR firms. When Mulcahy was asked to address the subject of selecting and keeping agencies he had this to say:

Overall, an agency is something special. It is not a supplier of raw materials or packaging. It is a partner and should be treated as such. It is neither a scapegoat nor an enemy. It is not the reason why relatively inexperienced managers don't get their work done. It is usually the reason they do.

An agency is an *outside* employee, not to be treated any differently than an *inside* employee. Guide them. Direct them. Listen to them. But mostly enjoy them. When selecting or evaluating an agency, remember how you as a client strive in relation to your agency counterparts.

Mulcahy coordinates and participates in his company's annual agency evaluation process. The criteria for evaluating performance of marketing public relations closely parallels the criteria Campbell Soup uses in evaluating its advertising agencies. It should be noted that while the client service criteria might be applied to other than marketing related public relations performance, some criteria, particularly those related to creative and new product work, apply only to marketing public relations.

The PR firm is evaluated on a scale of 1 to 5 on four criteria:

- Account team performance
- Management involvement
- Creative output
- New product work

Evaluation forms are completed by the principal client contact (or contacts if the agency represents more than one business group or more than one area of activity within the same business group). Mulcahy convenes a meeting of these evaluators with PR firm management and account team management. These annual meetings take place in the agency offices and usually last several hours. Two-way discussion is encouraged where the PR firm can openly discuss its problems and make suggestions for improving the relationship. The firm is also given the opportunity to respond in writing after the meeting.

The following evaluation form was used by Campbell Soup Company to evaluate the performance of its public relations programs with Golin/Harris Communications.

PR PROGRAM EVALUATION

Name of Agency _____   **Evaluator** _____

Product(s) _____   **Date** _____

Account Management

Rate on a Scale of 1 to 5
(5 Being the Highest)

1. Account people are well-trained public relations professionals. 1 2 3 4 5

2. Account team well organized. 1 2 3 4 5

3. They proact rather than react on marketing opportunities. 1 2 3 4 5

4. They have independent minds, conviction and are willing to express opinions. 1 2 3 4 5

5. They can develop sound strategies with equally sound rationales. 1 2 3 4 5

6. Follow-through on client requests are handled expeditiously. 1 2 3 4 5

7. Thoroughness, attention to detail in assignments. 1 2 3 4 5

8. Understanding of the business including competition. 1 2 3 4 5

9. Willingness to listen to and accept suggestions. 1 2 3 4 5

10. Cost consciousness. 1 2 3 4 5

11. Account team enthusiasm and involvement. 1 2 3 4 5

12. Account team cooperation with client. 1 2 3 4 5

13. Keeps client informed; effectively communicates. 1 2 3 4 5

14. Meets deadlines.   1 2 3 4 5

15. Competently plans for the long   1 2 3 4 5
    term.

16. Stays within budget.   1 2 3 4 5

17. Billing statements/invoices are   1 2 3 4 5
    prompt and accurate.

PLEASE COMMENT GENERALLY AND FREELY ON THE ACCOUNT MANAGEMENT TEAM.

_____

_____

_____

_____

_____

_____

Creative Output

1. Compatibility with overall strat-   1 2 3 4 5
   egies.

2. Acceptance of client suggestions.   1 2 3 4 5

3. Meeting timetables.   1 2 3 4 5

4. Cost consciousness.   1 2 3 4 5

5. Freshness of ideas/programs.   1 2 3 4 5

6. Management involvement.   1 2 3 4 5

7. Willingness to experiment.   1 2 3 4 5

PLEASE COMMENT GENERALLY AND FREELY ON THE CREATIVE OUTPUT.

_____

_____

_____

_____

_____

_____

New Product Work

1. Ability to develop public rela-   1 2 3 4 5
   tions strategies and programs.

2. Frequency of idea submissions   1 2 3 4 5
   and compatibility with product
   strategy/positioning.

3. Awareness of new product   1 2 3 4 5
   market/ target consumer.

4. Management involvement.   1 2 3 4 5

GENERAL COMMENTS IN THE AREA OF NEW PRODUCTS.

_____

_____

_____

_____

_____

_____

Overall Evaluation of Agency Performance

	Rate on a scale of 1 to 5 (5 Being the Highest)
Account Team Performance	1 2 3 4 5
Management Involvement	1 2 3 4 5
Creative Output	1 2 3 4 5
New Product Work	1 2 3 4 5

Specific Suggestions for Improvements in Any Selected Areas:

Account Management:

_____

_____

_____

_____

Creative Output:

_____

_____

_____

_____

New Product Work:

_____

_____

_____

_____

Other:

_____

_____

_____

_____

Performance Review Checklist

In preparing the 1991 A.N.A. monograph, Herb Zeltner reviewed several dozen evaluation forms currently used by clients and prepared the following checklist of common elements. Excerpts which follow from the section devoted to agency account service are most applicable to evaluating public relations performance.

- Do the people assigned to this account—senior, mid-level, and junior—have the appropriate background and familiarity to hold their own with their counterparts on our staff?
- Are they able to make a constructive contribution to our planning and executions?
- Do they add a broader dimension to our work, applying a wider perspective on marketplace developments from their experience elsewhere?
- Are they mature, sensible businesspeople with a good sense of proportion and mission?
- Are they familiar with our company, its objectives, and the particular market environment within which we find ourselves today?
- Do they work without prompting to learn more about our business and our company's operations so as to assist in planning and strategy work consistent with our needs?
- Are they knowledgeable about our competitors—their positioning, strengths, weaknesses, and strategic moves?
- Can these people relate our specific needs and requirements to new developments and innovative ideas occurring elsewhere so as to bring fresh thinking and totally new approaches to our work?
- Is our account team able to help us focus on our building–building priorities and resulting tactical needs and then provide direction and leadership or work alongside us in hammering out effective actions?

- Can they keep long-term strategic issues and short-term tactical matters in proper perspective and balance work accordingly?

- Are they successful in bringing adequate and appropriate agency resources from all required departments to bear on the assignment?

- Do they provide our company access to senior management or top talent in all disciplines as needed to help out at critical times?

- Do they anticipate crises and work to alleviate them? Are they "pro-active" in spotting opportunities and bringing them to our attention?

- Is the personality, style, and conduct of all key people working on our account an appropriate fit to our company and our way of doing business?

- Do people assigned to our account have a positive and constructive view of our business and our goals?

- Are they sensibly enthusiastic in moving things forward so that we all work toward common objectives in a positive, actionable manner?

- Are they sensitive to matters of confidentiality and concerned with security regarding proprietary information?

- Are my account people conscientious in meeting all due dates?

- Are they "buttoned-up" and good at organizing work lists and checking up on interim deadlines?

- Are they careful stewards of financial and budget matters, making certain that all charges are accurate, documented, reconciled, and in agreement with estimates?

- Do they make every effort to save funds and avoid overtime charges wherever possible?

- Is the quality and depth of staffing on my account—contact group and throughout the agency—an appropriate response to our needs?

- Is there reasonable stability in personnel—especially at senior levels—to assure continuity with people, systems, and requirements?

- Are training and development responsibilities well implemented so that people on our account grow in skill and understanding over time?

- Are recruitment, compensation, and promotion efforts effective in making good quality people available to our account—and keeping them on it?

- Is our account team responsive?

- Do we respect them and enjoy working with them?

- Is the agency disciplined in establishing strategic direction first and then addressing executional matters?

- Are they skilled at applying available market intelligence (both primary and secondary) so that strategic thinking is based on a solid, understandable foundation?

- Are their recommended strategies appropriate to our prospects and our categories of business? Are they logical, versatile, and sustainable over time?

- Is their strategic thinking fresh, compelling, effective?

- Is there a strong commitment to generating innovation and excitement in the creative effort?

- Are the tactics and specific approaches offered a correct outgrowth of strategic thinking? Do they "execute to strategy?"

The A.N.A. composite checklist for senior agency management applicable to PR firms includes these points:

- Do we get periodic updates on the agency as a whole—its structure, resources, health, and goals?

- Are members of the top agency management involved in our account to a reasonable and effective degree?

- Do they provide a total package of service and personnel appropriate to our needs, our size, and our position in their client roster?

- How specific is top agency management's knowledge of our current organization and the various market categories in which we operate? Can they advise and support us meaningfully in our management tasks as a result?

- Do they play a significant role in monitoring overall quality control at the agency, watching over their people's performance on our business?

- Is the personal "chemistry," style, and method of operation a comfortable fit for both parties? Is there stability in the relationship?

- Have they taken appropriate action as a result of earlier evaluations and suggestions for change?[3]

Criteria Checklist

Each client company has its unique corporate culture. Its expectations from its PR firms are a reflection of that culture. While some performance criteria are universal, other criteria and the weight assigned to each differ from company to company, culture to culture. Likewise, company policies and procedures which vary from company to company may significantly affect the agency-client relationship and therefore the means used to evaluate agency performance.

With that in mind, I have assembled the following checklist of 70 criteria used by several large and experienced clients to evaluate their advertising and PR firms. Some of these criteria overlap but are included here because the variations suggest shades of difference that may be more important in fact than in appearance. You may wish to adapt those criteria which are most appropriate to your situation.

HARRIS CHECKLIST OF 70 CRITERIA FOR EVALUATING ADVERTISING FIRMS

1. Background knowledge of markets and products

2. Initiative in developing facts and ideas

3. Evaluation of media placement

4. Understanding of public relations fundamentals

5. Overall administration

6. Responsiveness to requests

7. Cost consciousness

8. Quality of writing

10. Ability to make effective presentations

11. Maintenance of schedules and processing of paper work

12. Attention to detail

13. Use of research

14. Maintenance of contact

15. Personal initiative of account executives

16. Anticipates needs in advance of direction by client

17. Takes direction well

18. Adapts to changes in client's organization or needs

19. Makes reasonable recommendations of allocation of budgets

20. Contributes effectively to the development of new programs

21. Responds to client requests in a timely fashion

22. Submits alternate plans vs. a single plan

23. Has firm point of view

24. Produces fresh ideas and original approaches

25. Accurately interprets facts, strategies, and objectives into useable programs

26. Knowledge about the company's products, markets, and strategies

27. Produces on time

28. Performs well under pressure

29. Operates in a businesslike manner

30. Presents ideas not requested but felt to be good opportunities

31. Willingly accepts ideas from client

32. Keeps client up-to-date on relevant trends and developments

33. Provides client with regular review and analysis of competition's public relations program

34. Is efficient buyer of outside services and PR materials

35. Uses research in development of PR programs

36. Uses research to measure public relations effectiveness

37. Provides client with results and evaluation of public relations program

38. Billing procedures reflect a well-run internal accounting operation

39. Out-of-pocket expenses usually come close to cost estimates

40. Obtains competitive bids of work performed by outside suppliers

41. Maintains appropriate and adequate files for audit requirements

42. Public relations strategy is consistent with the marketing strategy and objectives

43. Public relations strategy arises from thorough analysis of business factors

44. Public relations strategy is clear and definitive

45. It establishes specific measurable goals

46. Recommended plan is clearly explained, well-documented, and on strategy

47. Plans are imaginative and innovative

48. Public relations firm implements its plans well

49. Agency is adequately staffed

50. Agency personnel is at high enough level

51. Continuity of account group

52. Knowledge of competitor's business

53. Ability to define and solve public relations problems

54. Use of research to establish creative direction

55. Quality of public relations materials prepared

56. PR firm management contribution to performance

57. Business acumen

58. Ability to handle workload

59. Desire to make a constructive contribution

60. Do what they say they'll do

61. Performance in keeping within budgets

62. Performance in winning awards

63. Follows company policies and procedures

64. Best agency people are on the account

65. Maturity and professionalism

66. Ability to involve key agency resources

67. Ability to communicate

68. Interest, enthusiasm, involvement in account

69. Open-mindedness

70. Ability to respond quickly

Two-Way Client-Agency Evaluation

More and more clients are using the evaluation process to foster a two-way dialogue in which the client evaluates the agency and the agency is given the opportunity to comment on the client.

A major packaged goods company asks its agencies to evaluate them as a client on the following ten criteria as excellent, above average, average, below average, or poor.

1. Are we the best client they have?

2. Do we really care?

3. Do we foster a true partnership based on mutual trust?

4. Do we ask for excellence?

5. Do we provide clear strategic direction based on consumer insight?

6. Do we look for the big idea?

7. Are our approval procedures streamlined?

8. Do we encourage personal involvement of top management of client/agency?

9. Do we take steps to ensure agency profitability?

10. Are we human?

The A.N.A. drew upon a number of forms which are used by clients to gain input from their agencies on how they are perceived. They generally consist of the following elements:

- Are goals set for the agency by the client businesslike, pertinent, and actionable?

- Are they stated as clearly and precisely as possible?

- Does client management allow reasonable "give and take" with the agency in establishing these goals?

- Do the people we deal with at the company secure orderly and effective direction and approval from senior management early enough in the program to minimize "wheel spinning," false starts, and later changes?

- Is senior management sufficiently involved in broad-range strategy matters so as to be well-informed throughout on how programs are initiated an implemented?

- Do the various members of the client organization provide clear and constructive responses and reactions to our recommendations and work?

- Are they professional, consistent, and objective in their opinions and views?

- Is the approval process clear-cut and working well?

- Are due dates reasonable and established far enough in advance to allow efficient deployment of our best agency resources?

- Have all steps been taken to streamline the process so the agency gets "course corrections" clearly, consistently, and early enough to respond properly?

- Is the interchange between client and agency personnel—at all levels—one of partnership and mutual trust?

- Is there a proper acknowledgement of expertise and experience on both sides?

- Is this an account my people want to work on?[4]

Agency Initiated Evaluations

Since many clients have no formal agency evaluation program, a number of PR firms have reversed the process by asking all of their clients to evaluate them on an annual or semi-annual basis. This process enables the agency to see itself as its clients do. It is used as a management tool to help agency management monitor the client–agency relationship. It provides a way for the agency to determine if their performance is meeting real client expectations. It also acts as an early warning system to identify problem areas in time for the agency to take corrective action before it's too late. Some clients have found it easier to respond to a questionnaire than to air their grievances in a constructive manner. In a flash, the agency can determine if it is meeting or exceeding client expectations or falling short.

PR firms using this type of evaluation form ask clients to rate them on such factors as:

- understanding client's business
- enthusiasm of the account team
- continuity of account team
- accessibility and involvement of PR firm senior management
- working well with client staff
- involving client in the program
- keeping the client well-informed
- listening to client

- not wasting client's time
- not waiting for client to initiate everything
- making client feel they are important to the firm
- returning phone calls promptly
- available and helpful when client calls
- dealing with problems openly and quickly
- good strategic thinking and planning
- creativity
- meeting deadlines
- results orientation
- measurement and program evaluation
- clear and complete bills
- budget management
- meeting or exceeding our expectations

By asking their clients how they are doing, agencies are able to effectively communicate their dedication to serving the client better. The message is that the agency cares enough to ask and is well focused on client service. The self-initiated agency evaluation process acts to reassure clients that they are in good hands.

The Net Net of Performance Evaluations

Most clients summarize their performance reviews by evaluating: (1) their agency's major strengths; (2) their major weaknesses; (3) major problems in the agency/client relationship; and (4) major accomplishments during the year. This leads to an overall evaluation of the agency's performance and recommendations for improvement.s a result of the process, the client should be able to determine if they have the right agency for the right job, if they are getting the best work and the best service that their public relations firm is capable of providing, if they are taking advantage of the agency's resources and experience, and finally, if they, the client, are part of the problem.

References

1. Ritchie and Shelley, "Making a Marriage Last: What Qualities Strengthen Client–Firm Bonds," 16.

2. *Evaluating Agency Performance*, (Association of National Advertisers, 1979).

3. *Evaluating Agency Performance*, Ibid.

4. *Evaluating Agency Performance*, Ibid.

CHAPTER 14

How to Not Get Fired

When Hal Riney, one of the most innovative and successful admen of our time, was asked to address the annual meeting of the Association of National Advertisers in 1988 on the secrets of his success, he did what all good creative men do. He turned the topic inside out and addressed the subject "How to Not Fire Your Advertising Agency." His observations on the things which can lead to a parting of the ways are every bit as applicable to client relationships with their public relations firms.

Riney points out that most agency selections seem to be made on the basis of a couple of two-hour meetings. He believes that is not nearly enough time to make a judgment about a firm the client is going to work with and depend on for years to come. He believes it's important for the client and agency to spend days, not hours, together to get to know each other well so that the decision is based on their up-close perceptions of the agency rather than formal presentations and speculative work.

He says that probably the next easiest way not to have to fire your agency is to ask your agency to proivde you with a group of people you're comfortable with.

> After all, agencies are nothing more than a bunch of people, some of whom are a hell of a lot better than others. And if you've got some of the lousy ones—or ones who, for other reasons, maybe aren't best-suited to handle your needs—ask the agency to make some changes.

Riney told the collected client that they should like their agency's work or at the very least be comfortable with it, but "if they're not, they should say so and get the agency to do something about it. It won't hurt us to hear the truth." He says that client–agency relationships would be a lot stronger and last a lot longer if each party had the confidence that the relationship wouldn't break down just because of a few rough spots now and then. He thinks that this way, people would be more open, more honest, and more committed to resolving problems than to fighting about them.

Riney believes that the great sin agencies commit is overpromising what they are going to accomplish and raising client expectations too high. Instead, he proposes that the client and agency agree on realistic goals, adding that while "this may cause a little discomfort in the short term, it's nothing compared to frustration and conflict that develops when the agency doesn't deliver what it said—and the client hoped—it would."[1]

Implications for PR Clients and Firms

All too often, PR firms are picked on the basis of a couple of meetings, maybe a briefing, and a presentation. That's not much time to get to know each other well enough to become engaged, much less married. That suggests the idea of long-term prospecting to PR firms and a willingness of clients to make time to hear unsolicited agency credentials presentations and less formal contacts. They might take a cue from their own purchasing departments whose job it is to be aware of available resources.

Getting to know the PR firm in depth means knowing not just the account team but agency management. From the agency side, this means not letting the account wither and die because of the failure of the account group to satisfy the client's expectations. Clients should know there is someone in the agency's high command they can take their problems to before they take their business elsewhere.

Then there is the matter of getting your money's worth—no more, no less. In my agency life, I observed that relations worked best when the agency was neither overpaid nor underpaid. Being underpaid is bad for account team morale and reasonable agency profit expectations. On the other side, clients don't like being taken advantage of and overcharged. Few PR firms deliberately overcharge for their services. More than likely, they lack systems to monitor staff time against budget. In either case, client–agency relationships, like real life marriages, can often be torn apart by dollars when good sense could and should prevail.

It has been my experience that the clients who get the best work aren't necessarily the largest but the ones that appreciate good work. My favorite clients said what they liked and what they didn't. I had the privilege of working with entrepreneurs like Charlie Lubin, founder of Sara Lee, who had no one to answer to. Another favorite client was Emmett Dedmon, then publisher of the *Chicago Sun-Times* and *Chicago Daily News*. Editors are used to making hundreds of editorial decisions a day. You always knew where you stood with people like them. Today, as Riney points out, "there are too many layers, too many lawyers, and too many people wondering what other people think."

How to Be a Good PR Client

David Finn, chairman and CEO of Ruder Finn, one of the largest independent public relations firms, and expert columnist for *Marketing News*, notes that a public relations agency can only be as good as its clients and that a difficult client makes it almost impossible to achieve effective results. He says that the good client should:

• *Respect the professionalism of the agency.* An impatient client may want fast results but they should recognize that PR people can't deliver on a predetermined timetable. PR people work through third parties like editors and government officials who have a public trust and need to invite their interest through an intelligent and knowledgable approach. Good clients understand the importance of this process.

• *Be a partner to the agency.* Good clients make an effort to work with the agency rather than have the agency work for them. This means working together in a collaborative way, recognizing the expertise of the PR person and, at the same time, bringing to the table a knowledge of what the company wants to accomplish. A great client is one who has a tendency to say "yes" to good new ideas. PR people live by ideas and a good client is careful not to squelch the creative impulse by constant negativism. Clients can maximize the effectiveness of the partnership by marrying their business judgment with an agency's creativity.

• *Do their best to respond quickly.* The day-to-day practice of PR often calls for a quick response. When a publication is planning an article, clients may have to agree to an interview on very short notice. Hesitation or belabored bureaucratic structures may result in lost opportunities. Press releases often have to be reviewed and approved quickly. This requires a "feel" for PR on the part of client management executives. It also means making time to discuss projects and review recommendations.

• *Like and be liked by the agency[2].* When an agency is selected in the first place, the most important consideration should be good chemistry. And that good chemistry has to be operative throughout the relationship if good results are to be achieved. This means respecting the way the other thinks and works, and enjoying the opportunity to be partners. It does not mean always agreeing with each other or never being critical. But people who like each other learn to resolve their differences amicably. They also want to do their very best to help accomplish their common objectives.

What Clients Expect

David Maister, whose Boston-based consulting firm specializes in the management of professional service organizations, has devised what he calls "The First Law of Service," expressed as a formula:

$$Satisfaction = Perception - Expectation.$$

He says that if the client perceives service at a certain level but expects something more (or different) then there will be dissatisfaction. He believes that the central challenge to service organizations including public relations firms is to manage not only the substance of what they do for clients but also to manage clients' expectations and perceptions. He says that it is common in the professional services sector that the professional does substantively superior work but that this is not perceived by the client because "the professionals are so completely oriented to their own values that the client's true needs are placed second."

Maister says that clients of professional firms want to know that they are not lost in the shuffle. They want to know that their matter is receiving the attention it deserves. The professional service firm that is adept at projecting a caring image and that backs that caring image with substantive reality, will do well in the marketplace. In other words, people don't care how much you know until they know how much you care.[3]

PR firms must recognize that client expectations vary widely from company to company. Some frame their expectations in terms of desired results. A PR executive of a major company responding to the Jack O'Dwyer survey on client attitudes toward PR firms cautioned fellow clients not to expect immediate results, adding that "the real payoff comes over a period of time." His advice: don't be quick to pull the trigger.

Others address their expectations in terms of the role they assign to the PR firm. Some clients expect the firm to act as counselor; others look to the agency primarily for implementation.[4] Ronald E. Rhody, senior vice-president for corporate communications, Bank of America, told *Public Relations Journal* that "with the large size of our corporate communications staff, we're not looking for public relations counsel—we're looking for work. We need a firm with the ability to listen carefully and understand what we want rather than what they want."[5]

On the other hand, Mary Moster, vice-president of corporate communications, Navistar International Corporation (formerly International Harvester) told the Counselors Academy of the Public Relations Society of America that she expects agencies to provide counsel that "challenges my thinking." She added that sound senior counsel "may be the single hardest thing to find."

Looking from the Inside

Moster, who was previously a senior vice-president with Hill & Knowlton, one of the largest international PR firms, says it's invaluable to see things from both the agency and client side "because while many things are similar, many things are very different." Because she has worked on both sides of the fence, her list of client expectations is particularly insightful. Her recommendations to counselors follow:

1. *Unbundle your services.* With the extreme cost pressure most corporate people face, they have to be very wise consumers of communications services. We're looking for specific expertise. We're looking for help on a specific project. We're looking, at times, for help from a specific person. Although I used to shudder, as an agency person, at the concept of the client "cherry picking" specific services or specific account staff, as the client I'm all for it. Bcause I am always pressed for time and for budget, I want to be able to access services as quickly and efficiently as possible. I have no time for services I don't need.

2. *Provide counsel.* A good counselor has: good critical judgment based on broad and deep experience; the ability to persuade and sell ideas; self-confidence born of experience; credibility with senior management; and brings a fresh perspective.

3. *You should know public relations better than I do.* You won't know my business better than I do but you can know what's happening in public relations better. You are exposed to a wider variety of clients and trends in public relations and business and know how to generalize those trends; know about changes in media and new technologies and are an expert in applying general information to specific situations.

4. *Provide leadership but don't get too far ahead of your client.* Be a source of creative ideas, bring in outside perspectives, bring fresh insights, but know your client well enough to know what is possible for that client. Be a source of ideas that work for them, not just those that worked for another client, and tailor your creativity to the client.

5. *Recognize what motivates a corporate communications person.* The influence of the CEO is an extraordinarily important factor. Does he want publicity? Does he work well with outside counsel? Is he looking to the public relations person for counsel? Recognize that the decision-making process is usually slower than in an agency; it often requires consensus and needs operating management buy-in. Recognize that budget constraints affect almost everyone and that there is a need to justify expenditures.

6. *Pay attention to little things.* This is not necessarily a strong point with people who choose to go into public relations. How the presentation looks does matter. Take care to get names right, keep mailing lists updated, avoid mistakes on bills.

7. *Give me value for my money.* In addition to implementing what the client needs, make sure you can provide value added. Know your strengths and be honest about what you can deliver. Are you really the best person to do this or are you just selling your company? You can be of more service to the company by telling them how to get things done, sometimes even with another supplier, such as a mailing house, than by attempting to do it yourself.

8. *Manage your business better.* When clients' budgets are under pressure, you are under pressure. You need to be better managers. You need to fix billing problems such as insufficient documentation, overcharging, and late billing. Lack of continuity of account staff is a big complaint. Don't use the client as a training ground. Staffing changes put pressure on the client. Your people should not be getting up to speed on my money. Big agencies should avoid squabbles about which office gets credit for billing; offices that don't trust each other and offices that sell against each other. Clients shouldn't be forced to get overly involved in how agencies manage their businesses. Increasingly, clients are going to hold agencies responsible for these things.

Moster also believes that PR firms should hold their clients to certain standards of performance. She thinks that PR firms should help their clients manage the relationship better by making sure that they:

- are provided with clear objectives
- are given an overall strategy or rationale for the project
- have the chance to meet with the key people involved
- know the budget
- are told how success on the project will be measured[6]

Lauer's Laws

Robert Lauer, vice-president of corporate affairs of the giant Sara Lee Corporation, who has held similar posts with Johnson Wax and Clorox and who has worked with public relations firms for many years, lists five critical areas in agency selection that he has dubbed **Lauer's Laws**.

Law #1. What the agency says is what the client ought to get. To get business and to keep it, you are going to have to be a good listener. Whenever the agency and client meet, the agency should start off with these questions: What do you want to tell me today? What do you want me to know? And then listen. Before leaving the meeting, the agency should insist on reviewing with the client what was decided. Then there's good chance that both parties will leave the meeting with an agreement and an understanding of what is supposed to happen next.

Law #2. A little knowledge is a dangerous thing, but it's a start. Everyone assigned to the account should become students of the client. They should know the client's business, its goals, its people, who its competitors are, and what they are doing. In order to build the relationship, the agency should insist on knowing everything they need to know to do an outstanding job and to become indispensable to the client. To keep the business, the agency must make the client feel that its people can't function effectively without them. It is part of the agency's job to help teach the client how to be a client. How the client assesses the agency's knowledge of business, problems, and needs is going to determine the level of confidence in the agency as consultant and counselor.

Law #3. A client/agency relationship is like a loaf of bread. No matter how you slice it, it's going to get stale. The PR agency has to work at keeping the relationship fresh. No client likes to be taken for granted or ignored. The agency should initiate meetings with the client to assess where things are. They should take the time to explain their billing system again. Clients go into shock when they get the agency's invoice each month. The agency needs to explain what the client is getting for the investment and why it is an important part of your overall client mix.

Law #4. Make sure your act is together before you take it on the road. The agency should be professional in everything they do. Every agency, regardless of how small, has a culture of its own and it's important that account people know that and understand and support it. The agency must train its people to supervise others before they can be promoted to a supervisory position. They shouldn't learn at the client's expense and risk losing the account. The agency should practice what it preaches.

Law #5. If a thing is worth doing, it's probably already been done. Clients are always looking for something original, something that's never been done before. The agency's job is to come up with that new idea, that variation on an old theme. Being creative is hard work, but somebody's got to do it. Clients expect PR firms to be creative in a way that responds to their needs.[7]

Client Expectation Checklist

Matthew P. Gonring, director of corporate communications at USG Corporation and adjunct professor in the master's program in corporate public relations at the Medill School of Journalism, Northwestern University, prepared the following checklist of client expectations:

1. Knowledge of client business
     take an interest
     Nexis, information banks
     regular review of company publications

history of client organization
culture
market positions
customer base
financial community perspective
employee make-up
audience characteristics

2. Developing supportive relationships
timetables
clear directions and understanding of what the client wants
Cadillac vs. Chevrolet
who will be doing the actual work
knowledge of internal capabilities
know your strengths
openness on costs—no surprises
cultivate relationships beyond communications department, if appropriate
see problem potential, address it

3. Value in communications counsel—depends on the voids, strengths of internal department
creativity
ideas
program development
research
knowledge of pitfalls
candid counsel
well read, who has done what
writing
community and professional networking/affiliations
media contacts
partnerships with other clients
specific expertise

4. Know your limitations
no agency can be everything to everybody

know when to direct elsewhere or recommend better use
of resources

knowledge of what you can do better than the client

what the agency should do vs. the client

media contacts—does the client have a greater likelihood
of success

be open about potential conflicts of interest[8]

Keys to Success

Kirk Stewart, president of Manning, Selvage & Lee, New York, summarizes the keys to a successful relationship in terms of fulfilled expectations. He lists the top five things a client should expect from its PR firm:[9]

- accurate estimates
- ability to meet deadlines
- truthfulness with expertise and results
- service
- high quality work

A PR firm, on the other hand, should expect these five things from its client:

- clear direction on the assignment
- prompt payment
- realistic deadlines
- honest feedback
- professional cooperation

Resolving Cultural Conflicts

Cleveland public relations counselor Bill Doll notes that differences in the unspoken expectations each side is operating under are the result of conflicts of culture. Doll says that "engaging a new client is as much of an anthropological exercise as it is a business one. To take on a new client is to sign on for an expedition into a foreign culture, one whose oddities and pitfalls are all the more treacherous because, on the surface, it all seems so familiar."

A major cause of conflict is clashing definitions about the place of public relations within the client's corporate culture. The client may never have worked with a PR firm before and may not know what public relations is or what they want the agency to do, or they may view public relations as a minor technical function—for example, only placing news releases with no broader strategic role. The consequences are real in the diminished scope and status of the field and in the conflict between the client's and the practitioner's view of public relations. Doll points out that at the other extreme are some clients that hold too exalted a view of public relations. They believe that public relations has magical powers, including controlling the media.

Other causes of cultural conflict cited by Doll include:

- the inaccessibility of the CEO to the PR firm and sometimes even to the internal communications person responsible for directing the agency's work

- hidden agendas and unacknowledged public relations objectives such as the glorification of the CEO or trying to advance the interests of a management faction or particular executive in a power struggle

- the siege mentality of a client who sees the media as the enemy, takes an adversarial stance, and has no interest in cooperating with reporters. The role of public relations is to clarify positions and change opinions. The stonewalling approach heightens antagonism and undercuts the PR firm's efforts.

- internal staff's fear of invasion when an outside firm is hired for the first time
    The firm threatens the internal staff's status, their work, and their jobs. The agency's key person may have a closer relationship with the CEO than the inside person, heightening the sense of jeopardy.

Doll says there is no simple formula for solving cultural conflicts short of bringing them into the open and engaging in forthright discussion about how the firm works, what it does, what to expect, and what not to expect. He concedes that other conflicts such as turf battles "are more resistant and may ultimately be fatal to a successful, long-term engagement."[10]

Client Concerns ... The Agency To Do List

Public relations management consultant James E. Lukaszweski believes that while most PR firms try hard to meet the expectations they believe their clients have, all too often neither the client nor the agency really address performance issues directly and in terms they both can understand. He has prepared the following list of 25 frequently expressed client concerns with recommendations for what the PR agency can do in response to each.

The Client Speaks Up

1. Don't make us pay for knowledge you should already have.

2. Anticipate the audiences we have and the questions your messages will create.

3. Big ideas are exciting, but they can be costly and the results are often unmeasurable. Please don't do it for the first time on our nickel.

4. Give us ideas, even in areas for which you aren't being paid.

5. If you pitch us with your principals, have them work on the account. Leave the rookies at home.

Agency *to Dos*

1. Learn the client's business.

2. Think in terms of the business rather than solely in terms of publicity and special events.

3. Be pragmatic. Promise only what you can deliver.

4. Show real intellectual curiosity, interest, and excitement about the product, problem, or organization.

5. Use professional staff who can write about and handle client issues in depth.

6. What we really want is creativity and execution. Save the rest.

6. Think creatively rather than waiting for assignments from a client.

7. Invest some of your human and financial capital in education and development.

7. Use training and research to create some concepts on your own nickel, not the client's.

8. Sometimes we feel as though there are only a limited number of ways to approach problems.

8. Try different approaches to different projects. Throw away the cookie cutter.

9. It would be great if creative people could really tie their ideas and plans to our strategy.

9. Understand, appreciate, and even utilize strategic planning techniques and tools.

10. We'd like a strategy that will help us win quickly.

10. Analyze trends so that your responses and actions seize the advantage in a situation.

11. What we really want is to be in the news *when* we want, *where* we want, saying what needs to be said.

11. Help clients determine how to make news, rather than seek publicity.

12. Just when we get to know your account people, they leave or get promoted, and we get new rookies.

12. Maintain close personal contacts. Make a people commitment to the account.

13. Could we really get into the *Wall Street Journal* or the *Times*?

13. Think unconventionally, even about how you select media. Offer the unsolicited proposal or idea . . . they are often winners.

14. We must find a way to have our internal people feel less threatened by our outside consultants.

14. Talk to, share with, and coach the people in the trenches, too. It's lack of personal chemistry that kills accounts.

15. What happens if it doesn't work?

16. How do the consultant's plans fit into our big picture? Can top management talk to them and actually communicate?

17. Every activity like this has to affect the bottom line in terms management will understand.

18. Too often, when we really need some quick advice, we can't reach you.

19. We'd like to know you're concerned about our business.

20. If we can't reach key people, no one else seems to be able to help us.

21. We have great meetings: too bad it takes weeks to get the ideas in a form for the rest of our management to review.

22. When we hold a press conference, the agency name comes up as often as ours.

23. Yeah, we've got ideas. But we're paying for your talent and experience.

24. When we're not sure if you really understand our situation, we're also not certain about what you think is our best course of action.

15. Actually have a plan B or C ready, which the client knows about and has approved.

16. Develop the ability to be generalists on business issues and topics. Ask to see and work with the strategic plan.

17. Add value to relationships and tasks. Build in effective measureability, reliability, and believability.

18. Be available, even after 5:00.

19. Check back frequently with clients, in good times and bad.

20. Build people depth into your relationship with the client.

21. Create and follow up on projects quickly, and in writing. Anticipate client management needs.

22. Promote the client, not the agency.

23. Be creative—don't just play back all the facts and ideas the client gives you.

24. Address issues using the *Concept of Completed Action*:
    a. Describe the problem effectively.
    b. Analyze it carefully.
    c. Develop appropriate options.
    d. Make at least one strong recommendation.

25. We like a positive, upbeat style, but cheeriness is not always appropriate!	25. Have more than one style. Some situations may require different people, experience, or people-to-people chemistry.[11]

Little Things That Mean a Lot

Ritchie and Spector point out that just like in a marriage, when the left-off toothpaste cap is enough to enrage, relatively minor matters in public relations can explode if not dealt with right away. They have drawn up the following checklist of everyday issues from both the client's and the firm's perspectives that can help both parties stay together.

Budgets:

To the firm: Don't waste the client's money on administrative support matters. For example, use cost-effective outside media list services and databases. Keep out-of-pocket costs to a minimum with no surprises. Show clients you are careful with their money.

To the client: Don't nickle and dime a firm about the retainer or out-of-pocket expenses. Don't allow them to lose money on your account. Review the budget often to see if it's on track, and if more funding is necessary to get the job done. The firm can help the client get a bigger budget next year.

Deadlines:

To the firm: Always meet your deadline. If it cannot be met, which should be rarely, notify the client ahead of time. A firm that misses deadlines consistently will be fired sooner rather than later.

To the client: Expect a lot but not the impossible. Most firms will try to move mountains for clients, work late nights and weekends to get the job done. But don't ask them to fulfill urgent requests too often—otherwise, the firm will feel it's being taken advantage of.

Approvals:

To the client: Enact and stick to a fast approval process. It's infuriating for firms to "hurry up and wait" when they prepare time-sensitive material. Also, keep to a minimum the number of people who have to review and approve.

Creativity:

To the firm: Only by thinking big, do big ideas emerge.

To the client: Encourage the firm to be creative and take risks. Dont' inhibit their thinking or imagination. Let them shoot for the stars. What might seem too unrealistic can be brought down to earth to conform to what's truly within reason.[12]

Making the Client Look Good

Paul Holmes, editor of *Inside PR*, says that the root of the problems between clients and their PR agencies is a "sometimes staggering level of ignorance on each side of the partnership." Clients too often don't understand what they are buying. They often expect quick-fix solutions and don't understand the need to provide PR people with access to senior corporate officers, including the CEO, and to corporate thinking. On the other hand, Holmes observes that PR firms often understand the media and the process of getting publicity better than they understand the inner workings of corporations. They fail to take into account the organizational politics that affect corporate decision making and fail to take the time to get to know the client's business and the business environment in which the company operates.

Former Searle PR chief William Greener, now a senior consultant with Fleishman-Hillard (one of the largest independent PR firms), says that there is one universal truism that applies to all clients.

> Every client wants an agency to make them look good. It is the one thing every client wants, even those that will not admit it. And to make a client look good you have to know the client, understand the client and his or her ambitions, responsibilities and desires. You have to understand the organization to which your client belongs and you

have to understand the underlying assumptions of your client. For some clients making them look good might mean the ability to obtain fifth-row center seats to <u>Phantom of the Opera</u> for the chairman and his wife. For others, it will be to run a program that produces more than 500 million media impressions.[13]

This behind-the-scenes glimpse at what really happens in some companies squares with my own experience. When I came into Foote, Cone & Belding to set up the agency's first public relations unit, I replaced a legendary PR director whose job it was to make the agency and its leaders look good in the advertiser community. I soon realized he had another job—getting tickets for shows and sports events for FCB executives and clients. I didn't win any popularity contests when I told the folks that I couldn't run a start-up business, serve clients, and run a ticket bureau at the same time.

Communicate! Communicate! Communicate!

The tendency of some PR firms to present themselves as all things to all clients has led to unrealistic expectations and unkept overpromises. Bill Greener says that an agency should decide what it wants to do well and what it doesn't want to do well. It should be willing to tell the client what it doesn't do, but that it knows people who do. Then it should tell them they would be best working with those people.

Eighty percent of the respondents to Ketchum Public Relation's survey of PR directors said they wanted their agencies to be more accountable and to be able to demonstrate their effectiveness in more quantifiable terms. More clients today expect their agencies to provide qualitative as well as quantitative analysis of their work.

Clients surveyed also emphasized the importance of a public relations agency that is prepared to question strategies and the assumptions that underlie them. Bob Berzok, public relations director at Union Carbide, told *Inside PR* that:

We want public relations agencies who are not afraid to tell us we are wrong when we are wrong. One of the things we are hiring PR agencies for is their advice and counsel, and they should feel free to give it. On the other hand, once we have decided to proceed with a course of action, for whatever reason, it is their job to go ahead with the implementation or to consider how they might be of use to the company in the future. Mutual trust is the basis for this kind of relationship.

Berzok says that most failures in client/agency relationships have come about because one party or often both was not clearly articulating what it wanted from the relationship.[14]

In the immortal words of Paul Newman in *Cool Hand Luke*, "what we have here is a failure to communicate." It's ironic that the breakdown in *communications* between a corporate communications department and a communications counseling firm is often the cause of a failed PR marriage.

Using the familiar marriage simile, Jack Porter, president of Porter–Novelli, describes this scenario:

> One day you get the feeling that the client is no longer telling you the whole story, is no longer taking you into his confidence. It's difficult to pinpoint why this happens and it's almost impossible to overcome.

Paul Holmes concludes:

> There is no doubt that the relationship between agency and client is most fruiful when both sides are communicating; telling the other party how they feel and are listening to the other party's feelings. Clients need to understand that public relations agencies are more effective when they are invited into the organization, given access to information and people beyond the client contact. Agencies need to understand the environment in which the client operates and they need to stop over-promising.[15]

Breaking Up Is Hard To Do

When all efforts not to get fired fail, it's time to cut bait. Gary Tobin of American Express says "don't stick with a firm when you know it's over. It's not fair to them. It's not good for you."

He offers these five rules for breaking an unsatisfactory relationship:

1. *Get personal.*   Notify the agency in person and in confidence before taking any further action. Follow up with a formal letter of notification that will activate whatever agreement you have for terminating the relationship. Don't start a search for a new agency until you've taken these steps.

2. *Agree on a story.*   Agree on what you'll tell people about the end of the relationship. It should be gracious and cast no blame. If the agency says one thing and you say another, it may sound like bad blood, which isn't good for either of you.

3. *Search confidentially.*   Trust the integrity of the old firm to work for you during the lameduck days while you seek a new firm. Using a consultant can keep your company name confidential during the preliminary stages, and help you avoid scores of phone calls, letters, and ambush meetings from eager PR firms you don't want to consider. The consultant can advise you about the capabilities of firms, contact them, weed out conflicts, and otherwise quality them for your needs and your style. That way, you can do much of the preliminary work behind the scenes and make your decisions before the word leaks out.

4. *Pass the baton.*   Don't just cut one agency off and bring the next one in cold. Let the old agency know you expect it to pass on the files in good order, giving the new agency a week or two for review of account activities. If possible, start the new agency on a new program before the old agency is released. This way, you'll have some continuity. Finally, take the time to educate the key people at the new firm.

5. *Don't do it too often.*   Changing agencies is chancy and it's a serious business. First, it's disruptive of your business. Second, it comes with no guarantees; the new agency may strike out as well. If you dump agencies at the drop of a hat, you not only risk missing the true cause of the problem, you may begin to run out of agencies well-qualified to serve your particular needs. And you'll begin to get a reputation for being a capricious client.[16]

References

1. "How to Not Fire Your Advertising Agency," Hal Riney address to Association of National Advertisers, 1988.

2. David Finn, "Want a Good Agency? Be a Good Client," *Marketing News* (undated).

3. David Maister, "Quality Work Doesn't Mean Quality Service," *American Lawyer.*

4. O'Dwyer's Services Report, 29.

5. "What Clients Seek in Public Relations Firms," *Public Relations Journal* (October 1990), 20.

6. "What We Expect of You—The Clients Speak," remarks of Mary C. Moster to Chicago PRSA Counselors Academy, June 4, 1991.

7. Robert Lauer address to PRSA Counselors Academy, April 1985.

8. "Client Expectations," remarks of Matthew P. Gonring to Chicago PRSA Counselors Academy, June 4, 1991.

9. *Jack O'Dwyer's Newsletter* (August 28, 1991) 6.

10. Bill Doll, "Avoiding Culture Conflict," *Public Relations Journal* (May 1991), 22.

11. James E. Lukaszweski, "The Perfect Agency," PRSA Counselor's Academy 1989 Spring Conference handout.

12. Ritchie and Spector, "Making a Marriage Last: What Qualities Strengthen Client–Firm Bonds." 16.

13. "The Key to a Perfect Relationship."

14. Ibid.

15. Ibid.

16. Gary Tobin, "How to Choose 'Em, Use 'Em and (When Necessary) Lose 'Em," *Inside PR's 1991 PR Agency Yellow Pages*, 13.

CHAPTER 15

Toward More Effective Client–Counselor Relationships

Andersen Consulting, the largest consulting company in the world, probably serves more clients than the top 100 public relations firms combined. They have literally written the book on client service and rewrite it daily to stay several leaps ahead of their clients. My firm, Golin/Harris Communications, for many years shared the Andersen Consulting public relations account with Burson–Marsteller. Burson is a $200 million public relations giant serving a worldwide client list of top clients several pages long. Their enviable record of success says something about their ability to work successfully with clients. Yet Harold Burson, the firm's founder–chairman, told me that he stays personally involved with this particular client because there are so many parallels between Andersen's business and the public relations agency business. These parallels are particularly applicable in maintaining high standards of quality service and managing relationships with clients.

Overcoming Resistance to Change

Michael C. Krauss, Andersen Consulting's director of marketing, points out that most people react to change, whether it is essentially positive or negative, as bad. He says that what usually stresses us as clients or counselors is the requirement that we do something different—that in effect, we change. To illustrate, he asked an audience of clients and counselors at the national conference of the Public Relations Society of America to consider how they personally would react to these hypothetical situations:

1. As a client, how do you feel when the agency introduces a new account representative?
2. As a counselor in a shop of broad-based generalists, how do you feel when the client demands a specialist?
3. As a client, how do you respond when the agency surfaces a "bold new idea" at the last minute?
4. As a counselor, how do you react when faced with the prospect of an agency account review?

Michael Krauss says that while much analytical work precedes an agency selection, in the end it comes down to professional judgment that is synonymous with faith. Initially, there is an act of faith involved that persuades us that together we can achieve our business and marketing objectives more effectively by working together. If we select our agencies and clients much the way we select our spouses, then the test of the relationship will ultimately come from how well we grow and prosper together. And that will depend on how well we respond to change.

He says that enduring client–agency relationships have certain shared characteristics:

• dedication to the highest standards of quality service
• commitment from the newest employee of the agency to the head of the office
• assignment of the best and brightest talent to the account team
• responsiveness
• enthusiasm
• big ideas
• reasonable pricing

- ability to be flexible, agile, and responsive in the face of growth and change[1]

Managing Change

Andersen Consultants has spent a great deal of time studying and researching the issues surrounding people's reaction to change. They operate on the premise that in order to manage change you need to understand its manifestations and its effects. In analyzing client response to the adoption of new technology, they find that a strong pattern emerges not unlike that in the agency–client relationship.

At the *arrival stage*, morale is very high, in some cases euphoric. Six to nine months down the road, the *engagement* phase is reached. The reality begins to set in. The initial promise of just how good it's going to be is just a bit tarnished. Then comes the third stage. In a PR context, the first major media placement has just backfired and the client is unhappy. This phase of the change curve is what Andersen calls the *valley of despair*. It's a trough all of us go through whenever we face change—personally, professionally, or organizationally.

In introducing information technology solutions to clients, Andersen has found over the years that the higher their initial expectations, the deeper the valley of despair and the more difficult it is to get to the *acceptance* phase.

Andersen asks its clients three questions which are equally relevant for public relations clients and counselors:

1. Can we change? Can we really do a better job as counselors and clients? We think that this is usually a question of economics. Frequently, we can't do any better because of economic constraints, but often we can.

From the client's perspective, this means asking yourself questions like:
Can we move from being penny watchers to wise investors?

Can we move from being short-term results oriented to long-term reward driven.

Can we move from being project focused to being relationship driven?

On the other hand, the agency should ask:

Can we change?

Can we stop being short-margin maximizers and become prudently profitable in the longer term?

Can we move from being short-term efficient to being long-term effective?

Can we stop competing on cost in the short term and compete on time and in quality in the longer term?

2. Should we change?   Frequently, we may want to change but social, cultural, or environmental forces may prevent or preclude us from change.

As clients:

Should we change from being oriented towards a division of labor with the agency doing this and the client doing that, to really creating a synthesis of effort?

Can we move from having closed, divided systems to having really open, organized, well-interrelated systems?

Can we move from being transaction oriented to create real transformations in our business?

From the agency's perspective:

Do we want to be merely reliable or do we want to create a cultural imperative towards responsiveness?

Do we want to move from being stable to really being agile?

Do we want to be process oriented or do we really want to become results oriented?

3. Will we change?   Often, we may want to change. Economically, we may be able to change. The culture may permit us to change. But whether or not we actually will change is a function of individual leadership, commitment, and even personal courage.

As clients:

> Are we going to move from being short-sighted to really being visionary?
>
> Are we going to move from being bureaucratic to being decisive?
>
> Are we going to move from being conservative to being really innovative?

As agency executives:

> Are we going to be set in our ways or are we really going to be farsighted?
>
> Are we going to be arrogant or are we going to be trustworthy?
>
> Are we going to be conventional or are we going to be resourceful?

Prescription for Relationship Management

Michael Krauss suggests that public relations clients and counselors apply some of the following conclusions, prescriptions, and suggestions to improve their relationships:

1. Awareness. Are you considering the issues of relationship management?

2. Are you giving and receiving consistent, honest feedback?

3. Do you have a specific action plan for developing and growing the relationship?

4. Vision. Do you have a conceptual idea of where you want the
   client and agency relationship to go?

5. Are you managing the relationship in view of the three Ps: the professional, personal, and political dimensions of relationships?

6. Change management. How will you keep pace and adjust effectively as clients and counselors to be in tune with the ever increasing rate of change?

7. Understanding. Do you really have a mutual understanding of one another's business?

8. Trust and balance. Have you created a relationship built on trust and balance that will last? Are you moving away from adversarial situations and towards balanced relationships?

Making It Work

Making the client–counselor relationship work requires mutual trust and respect, a commitment to open communication, and a recognition that neither partner has a monopoly on truth. Despite frequent references to the client–agency relationship as a "partnership," you (the client) are the boss. You set the pace. It's your program and it's your money. If you build a relationship with a PR firm based on trust and balance, you will get your money's worth and then some.

It is the way for the PR firm to not get fired. It is the way for the client to avoid repeating the costly, time-consuming process of choosing a new PR firm.

The client that chooses its agency well to begin with and is dedicated to making the relationship work can look forward to a long and mutually rewarding business life with its PR firm.

References

1. Thomas L. Harris and Michael C. Krauss, "Effective Counselor and Client Relationships: How to Get the Most Value for the Least Investment Out of Your Public Relations Firm," presentation to Public Relations Society of America Annual Conference, November 15, 1988.

PRSA Corporate Section Members Look at Public Relations Now and Down the Road
A Survey for the Counselors Academy
Conducted by Savitz Research Center, Inc., April 10, 1991

Attitudes Towards and Usage of Outside Counselors

About the Survey
- Method - Mail
- Universe - PRSA Members in the Corporate Section
- Outgoing - 1,253 (February 25–26, 1991)
- Returns - 263
- Response - 21% (March 25, 1991, cut-off)

Usage of Independent Counsel

	Total Sample
Annual contract	22%
Regular assignments, but no annual contract	9
As needed, depending on work load	23
Special assignments (unusual, unforeseen need)	21
Do not use outside counsel now	26
No response	2

Base: 263

Among Those Who Use Outside Counsel . . .
- They deal, on average, with 2.4 firms
- Almost 3 out of 10 (29%) were engaged for the first time in 1990

185

Reasons for Taking On New Firm

	Those Engaging New Firm in 1990
Specialist with capabilities not available among other counselors	54%
An addition to outside resources	34
Replace an incumbent	13
Other reasons (special event, first time use of outside counsel, crisis, etc.)	22

Base: 91   (Multiple responses accepted)

Competitive Bidding Practices

Yes	18%
No	47
Depends on nature of assignment	35

Base: 91

Attitudes Towards New Business Solicitations from Counselors

	Total Sample
Will see firms that approach on a selective basis	55%
Will see any accredited firm that approaches	4
Do not accept new business solicitations	37
Don't know/No answer	4

Base: 263

Criteria for Selecting Independent Counsel in a Competitive Environment

	Average Score	Top 2 Boxes	Bottom 2 Boxes	Gap
Ability to meet deadlines	9.3	78	1	+77
Key account people assigned	8.8	63	1	+62
Experience in a particular subject	8.6	53	1	+52
Perception of "fit"	8.6	56	1	+55
Reputation of the firm	8.5	53	2	+51
Experience in your industry	8.3	51	2	+49
Stability of firm's staff	7.9	32	★	+32
Financial stability	7.7	34	2	+32
Fee structure	7.5	30	3	+27
Independent references	7.5	29	3	+26
Firm's presentation to you	7.3	26	3	+23
Geographic proximity	6.8	26	8	+18
Examination portfolio	6.3	15	7	+8
References furnished by firm	6.2	15	8	+7
Years in business	5.5	5	9	−4
Size of firm	4.4	3	21	−18

Base: 263

Verbatim Responses to Savitz Research Survey for the Counselors Academy

Following is a selection of verbatim advice offered to PR films soliciting the business of clients participating in the study.

Under-promise, over-deliver—thereby demonstrating there is something about our business you cherish.

The best PR firms I have run into have demonstrated the valuable ability to anticipate my needs. Some may call it luck—which is when proper preparation meets opportunity.

Do your homework, know who we are and something about our problems, make relevant, helpful, creative recommendations for potential solutions.

Approach us with an open mind, rather than a "my way is the best way" mentality.

Understand that PR is not exclusive, it's part of marketing—so you'd better understand my business, my customers, my niche.

Offer "relevant" credentials, expertise and experience—don't cold call and don't fake it.

Tell the client exactly which people will be assigned to the account and stick to it. Don't "bait and switch."

Deliver on your promises. Don't promise capabilities you do not possess. Differentiate yourself.

Identify what our company most needs and sell that rather than just showing protfolio "hits."

Do your homework. Don't expect us to do it for you. Listen carefully to what the assignment is so that you don't do what we don't need.

Don't try to sell me a Cadillac when a Chevrolet will do just fine. Clearly identify who would work the account rather than the titled gentry. And have people who can write intelligently.

Take the time and effort to understand the business and the needs of the organization. I'm tired of seeing cookie-cutter presentations where firms try to fit clients into those areas they can easily bill. Be problem-solvers in the true sense of the word.

Know who you are and what you do. Don't promise "media hits." If you can't provide a specific service, tell me.

Understand our internal problems and show me how something else can be done better and more cost effectively. Don't try to sell me something I am already doing.

Do homework, research our goals and objectives and offer a fresh idea or new approach. We know our basic problems. If you come up with a great solution, we'll listen.

Don't strut your stuff too much. Be honest, on time, professional, creative. Learn my business if you want to serve it.

I would recommend that a firm suggest ways to work with the company's PR staff to enhance what they do—not try to take over the PR function.

Be able to convey that you are an agency that does what you say you'll do when you say you'll do it. Service the client as no one else can.

Know the business you're soliciting. Don't parade a lot of successes that have absolutely no relevance to the firm being pitched.

Learn our culture and our values.

Give me a sense of perspective; what can you do that is of value to us; what are some of your results-oriented successes for others?

Your presentation is the first time I see you in action. Tell me how our relationship will work from project initiation to completion. Be honest about your strengths and limitations.

Make sure your PR firm effectively communicates how clients' needs are prioritized; reassure my company that experienced, reliable professionals will be working on our account.

Be prepared, be honest, be straightforward, be friendly, be confident without being cocky.

I'm turned off by superficial reps who think they know what we do and launch an elaborate pitch that only shows they have no clue what our business is.

Don't make a "hard sell" to the point where it becomes offensive. Show me how you can help and then respect my time lines.

Go for the small projects first and try to establish a long-term relationship. Demonstrate expertise and gain trust.

You must be able to provide me with services I cannot provide by simply adding more support staff.

During your presentation, carefully balance your claim to expertise in PR program development with knowledge and particular business expertise of solicited company's management.

Presentation skills and professionalism are key requirements. The agency will be conveying the image of the client.

If you've never done it before, don't try to sell it to me.

Excel in a niche or two in addition to general counseling ability. Align your people carefully with corporate counterparts.

Keep a conservative profile; don't push.

Go for a start-up project; don't try for a "home run."

Forget blue sky projects; keep focused on work that affects and impacts our business results or influences our business environment.

Index